SECRET OF THE SIDDHAS

Swami Muktananda

CONTENTS

BHAGAWAN NITYANANDA

INTRODUCTION

When, twenty-four years ago, Swami Muktānanda became a fully realized master, a Siddha, it was an interior event, requiring no certificates or public titles. He simply knew it, he has said, as certainly and profoundly as one knows physical pain, or overwhelming love. His Guru, Swami Nityā-nanda, built a small house for him in the nearby township of Gavdevi, a cluster of mud and straw huts in a valley north of Bombay. Nityānanda would send visitors to him from his Āshram in Ganeshpuri, half a mile away, and Muktānanda would answer their questions, translating Nityānanda's cryptic utterances into plain language. From the first, therefore, Muktānanda was a teacher, an expounder of secrets. Speaking of those years, Muktānanda says that Nityānanda simply told him to live there, that was all, and he obeyed his Guru. Even after Nityānanda died, Muktānanda went on living in the small house. He grew a rose garden and cooked meals for the growing number of visitors who had begun to suspect that he was more than an intelligent and well-spoken yogi, that he was, indeed, the heir to Nityānanda's power, his spiritual son, a Siddha.

I see Baba Muktānanda through the eyes of devotees who knew him in those years, at work in his rose garden or speaking with the visitors who came on weekends. He talks about Kabīr, Tukārām, and Jnāneshwar, singing their great poems not simply as literature, but as the expression of an experience he knows deeply and completely, for it is his own. I see an absorbed, vigorous man, firm in the daily delight of living according to his Guru's instruction, even when that instruction meant reversing the pattern of a lifetime. For Muktānanda had spent almost twenty-five years wandering the roads of India. Ever since an austere *avadhūta* named Nityānanda had patted him on the head while visiting his school in south India, Muktānanda, then a fifteen-year-old boy named Krishna, had been possessed of a deep desire, amounting to a passion, to meet holy men. He wanted to acquire for himself the knowledge they possessed which, for all their personal differences and eccentricities, gave each of them the same radiant power, as if one Self peered through all their acts. In *Secret of the Siddhas*, Muktānanda pays tribute to the *avadhūtas* and Siddhas he met during those years: Zipruannā, Ranga Avadhūt, Siddhārūda Swāmi, Kabīr Das, and Hari Giri Bābā are only some of the great beings to whom Baba expresses his gratitude for having given him glimpses of the Self in all its playfulness, even when he was still seeking it, not yet knowing how patiently the Self sported in the solitude of his own being.

Half a lifetime later, Muktānanda met his Guru halfway across India and found that he was the same *avadhūta* who had started him on his search long before, Nityānanda, now living beside a hot sulfer spring in a jungle valley. The valley was alive with activity, for Nityānanda's fame had stirred the people of the surrounding countryside. They cleared roads, built houses, created villages, an Āshram, a hospital, schools, all as service to the enigmatic holy man they loved.

Here begins the story Baba has told in his spiritual autobiography, *Play of Consciousness*. It is the story of a disciple and a master, of an inner journey as surprising and exciting as an adventure story. Above all, it is the story of a stubborn, loving soul being tested and triumphing because, by an alchemy of self-change which is at the heart of Siddha Yoga, he had wedded his inward being to his Guru so completely that he had become his Guru. This oneness, he has said, is the goal, and the entire teaching, of Siddha Yoga. As the philosopher Sören Kierkegaard wrote, "He who does the work becomes his own Father."

Since then, years have passed. The original house in Gavdevi is now part of a large building surrounded by other buildings in what has become a large Ashram called Gurudev Siddha Peeth. Baba's rose garden has become a lovely park. A town is springing up around it. Busloads of pilgrims come from all over India to see Baba and have his *darshan*, as he himself, years before, had walked all over India to have the *darshan* of great beings. Yet I still see Baba as I imagine he was in that early time, living with the casualness and simplicity of a happy man, not "doing" anything, simply following his Guru's word: Live here, that's all. I remember the story an American disciple told me about a celebration that took place at Gurudev Siddha Peeth several years ago. Thousands of visitors were arriving; tents were being erected on open ground all over the Āshram, even on rooftops. Everywhere preparations went on in a great clatter of activity. Sitting on his porch, Baba turned to this disciple and said, "You see, I'm just going to sit here, twirling my stick, but everything will get done." And as always, it did. I have never ceased to have that image of Baba: sitting casually, twirling his stick, in Ganeshpuri or New York, alone or surrounded by thousands of busy devotees, speaking in Carnegie Hall or talking to a single person in his garden. Just twirling his stick but, with steadiness and grace, becoming a center around which activity whirls: "a hub of the wheeled universe," as Walt Whitman wrote.

In Sanskrit, a fully realized master is called a Paramahamsa, a supreme swan, and the symbol is expressive. A swan embodies self-control, in-gathered power, muscular elegance, whether it wheels overhead or moves, stately and silent, over the water. A swan is intensely fascinating. When it swims, it seems immobile, like a yogi locked in meditation. Such is a Paramahamsa: perfect, not as a work of art, but as a living being whose perfection includes feelings and a living body and is therefore close to us, as an idealized image can never be.

At the heart of Siddha Yoga is the relationship with a Siddha, a Paramahamsa, who gives *shaktipāt*. A Siddha teaches that consciousness itself is perfection, containing thoughts and worlds, expanding to include all of time and space or contracting to a single blade of grass. Emotions dart within it, Baba has written, like a bee alighting on the different petals of a flower. In the course of our lives, we become creatures of change. Our minds flutter like butterflies in the stillness of a field. A Siddha's steadiness reminds us of the field of God. His stillness erupts within us, and suddenly we are stunned by the shift in our minds. We are, momentarily, free. *Shaktipāt* has propelled us into the mind's stillness where we are enthralled, not by the objects of consciousness, but by consciousness itself, which resembles a sky, overarching and blue. This is a Siddha's gift, the very gift he himself received from his Guru and which he passes on, intact, to us. Siddha Yoga consists of this: the heart's gift of a great being received by his disciple who, by receiving it, discovers that he is equally great, equally conscious.

In the Siddha tradition, this gift is called *shaktipāt*, and to call it a gift is only partly accurate. For Baba insists that *shaktipāt* is not his to give or withold: *Shaktipāt* is taken as much as it is given. It is a kind of holy theft. The disciple's stubborn desire, and his readiness, take it, and the Siddha, happy to have been found out, lets it go. Baba calls this "disciple's grace." A Siddha exists to be found out, and he does everything in his power to help his disciple. He reveals his "secret" in every way he can so that the disciple, not merely hearing words and thoughts, hears the deep tone of knowledge, and is changed. In this sense, the "secret" is not any recipe or formula which the Guru imparts. It is not the subject of a previously concealed text. Truly speaking, the "secret" lies with the disciple, not the Guru. It is the place of that interior passage through which merely verbal knowledge eludes the mind's changeable nature and plunges to the heart. The Guru is expert at finding this passage and unlocking it, so that the disciple, hearing what is said, hears with all his heart, perhaps for the first time.

Among the stories Baba tells, there is one which expresses the "secret" of this most profound kind of learning with particular beauty and simplicity. Once a man named Hamid went with a friend to see Baba Musa and ask if he would accept them as disciples. Musa agreed and said, "You can start working in those fields over there." Hamid and his friend did what Baba Musa told them to do. For two years, they worked punctually, with great love, from eight o'clock in the morning until eight o'clock at night. But after two years, Hamid's friend began to think, "What's so unusual about this field? I have a field of my own; I could work there and consider that, too, to be service to the Guru." With these doubts in his mind, he left.

Meanwhile, Hamid thought, "I'm serving the Guru already; why don't I wait and see what happens?"

So Hamid went on with his work, and as he did he became more and more interested in what he was doing. He began to feel a contentment within himself, and this contentment in turn increased his interest. As his work became more satisfying, he stopped thinking about the hours he was spending, for he had begun to see that *seva*, or service to the Guru, was the supreme means to peace. He became so absorbed in his task that what had merely been work was not work to him

anymore; what had been a field was not just a field. His *seva*
had become a divine apprenticeship. He understood now
that *seva* was not just *seva*; it was a way to immerse oneself
in God through one's work. Thus, *seva* itself was a technique.
When Hamid realized this, he became extremely happy.

During all this time, he kept thinking about his Guru, until
one day he decided to go to him again. When Baba saw him
coming, he said, "Well, Hamid, is your work finished?"

"No, I'm still doing it," Hamid answered.

"Well, it's completed now. You can go. But remember:
Everything is knowledge; everything is instruction. Wherever you become immersed in your *seva*, you will receive
inner wisdom." Saying that, he sent his disciple away.

Hamid left and went to Turkestan, where he decided to
settle. As time passed, his *seva* took the form of knowledge
and resided in his heart. He became a man of knowledge, and
thousands of disciples came to study with him. He, in turn,
made them perform *seva* to become aware of the majesty of
the Guru. Hamid's fame spread far and wide. One day the
friend who had first come with him to see Baba Musa heard
stories about a powerful holy man in Turkestan. He decided
to visit this holy man and see what he could learn from him.

Upon arriving at Hamid's ashram, he recognized his old
Guru-brother. He remembered how he had once done *seva*
with Hamid for two years, and now here he was, a great
being.

"Brother, how did you attain this divinity?" he asked
Hamid. "What secret did Baba Musa impart to you after I
left?"

"Brother, Baba Musa didn't teach me any secret after you
left," Hamid answered. "I just went on working in the field,
and as I did, knowledge began to arise in me. I didn't have to
sit with my eyes closed and meditate. I experienced a state of
meditation even while I was working. I began to have glimpses
of ecstacy and love and became increasingly immersed in

them. I saw the Supreme Consciousness pervading the entire universe. I saw Baba Musa in myself, in cows, and in trees; I saw him in people. I saw that everything was God, or Baba Musa, or myself and became ecstatic in the experience of the divine."

Such is the vision Baba gives us of the Guru's teaching, which is not concerned with personal advice, or complicated rituals, or burning the right kind of incense, but with a mysterious form of self-concentration called *seva*: service to the stillness in one's mind; service to the Guru, who is the mirror of Consciousness; service to humanity; service as an act both of love and of self-reliance, turning one's very life into a form of meditation.

Baba has often said that blind faith is an enemy of the Guru–disciple relationship. Not only should a person examine a master carefully before accepting him in order to know whether his life and his teaching are truly one; he should be self-aware and observant, even as a disciple. For me, the unfailing sign of Baba's authority as a teacher is the bold simplicity of what he writes and says. In everything he does, there is a tone of certainty and direct knowledge. Baba loves clarity. He writes as he speaks: urgently, generously, appealing not to theologians and philosophers, but to the elementary humanness in each of us. He tells us that knowledge is a form not only of thinking, but of living. He says, "God dwells within you as you," and means the you which exists at the deepest level of your being, as the Self. Clarity is the language of the Self, and it is Baba's language.

Secret of the Siddhas is written in this tone of knowledge. It touches on every aspect of Baba's teaching, from practical instructions on diet and the practice of meditation to the nature of the inward experience as he has known it. In Book I, "The Yoga of the Siddhas," he writes about the great beings who meant so much to him and exhorts his disciples to understand their example. He writes about Nityānanda, from whom all his knowledge flows and to whom all his work is dedicated.

Book II, "The Philosophy of the Siddhas," deals with an aspect of Baba's teaching on which he has placed increasing emphasis in recent years: the philosophy of Kashmir Shaivism. This incomparably subtle branch of Indian thought is devoted to presenting a practical psychology of liberation. It offers a manual of the stages of learning, signaling the resistances the individual encounters as his mind clings to its limitations, even while the pull of the Self urges him onward. The terminology of Kashmir Shaivism is precise and technical. Although its language can at times be difficult for the layman, the underlying wisdom of the Shaivite sages is remarkably pungent and straightforward.

The *Shiva Sūtras* and the other principal texts of Kashmir Shaivism, such as the *Spanda Kārikā* and the *Pratyabhijñāhridayam*, offer in compressed, sometimes enigmatic form a map of the divine, combined with a practical concern with Self-realization. At the heart of the process of self-change called *sādhanā*, the Shaivite system places the clarifying presence of the Guru, a fully realized master who, as the *Shiva Sūtras* state, is considered to be the means to liberation. Over the centuries, successive masters have enriched the canon of Shaivite thought, as is customary in India, by means of commentaries on the original texts. This tradition of commentary has resulted in a body of scriptural writing that is alive and changing because it is grounded ever-anew in the experience and thoughtfulness of Siddhas. In "The Philosophy of the Siddhas," Baba has cut through the technical overlays of Shaivite philosophy to reveal its essential core as clearly as has ever been done. Kashmir Shaivism, as Baba describes it, revels in the play of multiplicity and oneness which is the world. God is everywhere; He is everything. The world in its variety is not an illusion to be rejected. This eruptive and beautiful world is God's exuberance; it is God bursting into form. Individuality as we know it is merely a contracted form of God. In our condition as contracted individuals, we have forgotten that the many is also One and the One is also many. To remember this at that inner point of our beings where intellect and experience merge is to become that very One. It is to become God. Baba writes, "The universe is a garden for us to roam in with love. It is not intended as a source of attachment, jealousy, hatred, or anxiety. These only destroy our equanimity. Give up all desires. If something comes, let it come; if something goes, let it go. It is all Shiva's play. This is not a mere universe; it is the image of Him. Knowing it as Shiva, love it. Meditate on the awareness that all conscious beings as well as inert matter are Shiva. Having the knowledge of Shiva, understand that the world is the embodiment of Him."

Thus, in the two parts of *Secret of the Siddhas*, Baba is first a *bhakta*, a devotee of God, writing with love and enthusiasm about God's inner kingdom in the tradition of the poet-saints whose works he sings; then he is a philosopher, clarifying and renewing the ancient tradition of Kashmir Shaivism. Together, these form the substance of the Siddha tradition, of which Baba's life and thought are a profound example. By presenting these subjects with such clarity and love, he makes it possible for us not only to understand them but to absorb them deeply and completely into our lives.

PAUL ZWEIG

Paul Zweig is a poet and essayist, author of such books as The Adventurers *and* Three Journeys, *and head of the Department of Comparative Literature at Queens College, New York.*

AN APPRECIATION

I am very impressed by *Secret of the Siddhas*. The subject is deep and profound, but Baba has presented it so simply that even an ordinary person can easily understand it. There is clarity in Baba's thoughts, and therefore there is no obscurity in his language and style. One reads the book with great delight.

The Shaivism of Kashmir has not yet been widely disseminated. Generally it is considered to be beyond the understanding of the public, and therefore people have not given it much attention. Therefore, by writing this book, Baba has done a great service. Those who read it will obtain complete knowledge of this great path, and I am sure that in this way the book will help its readers to reach the final goal of all paths.

For this I heartily congratulate Baba and offer him my grateful thanks.

YASHPAL JAIN

Yashpal Jain is the author of numerous books of essays and short stories, as well as the editor of a prominent literary magazine in Delhi. He has twice received the prestigious Soviet Land Nehru Prize for his writing.

SWAMI MUKTANANDA

INVOCATION

Because he exists everywhere at all times,
        he is called eternal.
Because he is without taint or defect, he is called pure.
He constantly pulsates with bliss in the hearts of all.
This work, *Secret of the Siddhas*, was born
        through the inspiration of
        Nityānanda, the Self of all.

O Lord! Through your grace, even the unintelligent
        can understand philosophy.
Through your touch, a seeker has the vision of the Self.
Although you are everywhere, you dwell most specifically
        in the heart of a human being.
I have come to know that you alone exist in conscious
        beings as well as inert matter.

O Guru! In *Secret of the Siddhas*, you alone dwell
        in delight.
You alone permeate all letters, words, and the art of poetry.
Without you, the world does not exist.
Muktānanda, know this to be true.

Note on the Translation

Yoginī Shrī Malti Devi

This work of literature was written by Swāmi Muktānanda in Hindi in his own hand. Yoginī Shrī Malti Devi translated it into English with great effort. Swāmi Prajnānanda, Swāmi Samatānanda, Swāmi Kripānanda, and Ma Durgānanda helped with the editing.

Definition of Sanskrit Terms

All Sanskrit words, as well as terms that may be unfamiliar to a Western reader, are defined in the glossary except where an explanation of their meaning is essential to one's understanding of the text. In such cases, they are defined either in the text or in footnotes.

Transliteration of Devanageri Script

A diacritical mark has been used to indicate the long vowel sounds in Sanskrit words, for example, ā, ō, ū. Otherwise, for the sake of simplicity, all other diacritics have been omitted.

Book I

Yoga of the Siddhas

1

The Heart of Siddha Yoga

1. Siddha Yoga and meditation on the Self do not oppose any religion, sect, or code of ethics.

2. This meditation revolution does not violate the laws of any government.

3. It is not against any caste or social class.

4. It does not argue with either the good or bad qualities of any country.

5. This meditation revolution is opposed to hatred among people, lack of consideration, ignorance, indolence, and falsehood.

6. This Siddha Yoga revolution endeavors to establish industriousness, to bring about oneness on the earth, knowledge, a search for the inner Consciousness, and the attainment of one's own Self.

1

7. This Siddha Yoga revolution is founded on high principles. It is an invitation to universal brotherhood. Because light, truth, and peace exist in all, we should love one another with respect for the Self in all.

8. Siddha Yoga takes no interest in differences. It does not argue about bigotry or cults. In Siddha Yoga, there is no room for cultism. Siddha Yoga is the same as it was thousands of years ago at the creation of the universe. Then there were yogis and great sages who had transcended their minds, and Siddha Yoga was born from their arduous *sādhanā* and ultimate perfection. Siddha Yoga is the teaching of those great beings who had fully attained the Truth and who had become one with Paramashiva, the all-pervasive Consciousness and Supreme Guru. This field of knowledge is beyond human ambition, beyond the mind and imagination. It is a venerable path to the realization of Truth. We follow it seeking the supreme love of our own inner Consciousness.

9. The main task of Siddha Yoga is to unfold fully the God-consciousness which lies hidden in all human beings. It culminates in the experience of "I am That" — the experience of our identity with God — and in the attainment of our own inner joy. Siddha Yoga destroys our negativities; it removes the dullness and lack of clarity of our minds; and it eradicates the differences among religions, people, and colors. By respecting all, Siddha Yoga dispels the hatred that continually arises in the world.

10. The task of Siddha Yoga is to put an end to the notion of duality — to distinctions of high and low, superior and inferior, rich and poor — to arguments and disputes, to the race-track competition among people, and to the futile rush-

ing toward a dream of progress. Siddha Yoga enables one to make the journey through the world with supreme bliss.

11.   Siddha Yoga teaches: "May all people everywhere live happily and peacefully. May everyone become free of hatred, jealousy, and enmity. May no one see pain, even in a dream." Siddha Yoga is the abode of love for all.

12.   In Siddha Yoga, we attain the knowledge of our birth-right.

13.   Siddha Yoga nurtures one who wants the good fortune of reveling in the delightful game of the inner Self. Through it, one attains inner joy and achieves fulfillment in life.

14.   Through the pursuit of Siddha Yoga, the inner conscious energy called Kundalinī is awakened; yogic movements, or *kriyās*, automatically occur; and this great energy is fully unfolded.

15.   A seeker experiences this energy within him as having complete knowledge of all spiritual practices. In the *kriyās* of Siddha Yoga, there is no danger.

16.   Siddha Yoga affirms that the individual soul is nothing other than the Absolute. There is not the slightest difference between the individual and God.

17.   Because the Self identifies itself with the mind, then the senses and the physical body, it is called the experiencer.

When it comes in contact with the powers of action,[1] it calls itself the doer. When it comes in contact with the senses of perception, it calls itself the perceiver. Through its attachment to the body, it undergoes birth and death.

18. Through Siddha Yoga, the Self attains the knowledge of its true nature and immortality. It becomes aware, "I am deathless."

19. When the inner energy is awakened through Siddha Yoga, a seeker may immediately experience a surge of extraordinary bliss and ecstasy.

20. In Siddha Yoga, Kundalinī is called Chidānanda-lahari, the wave of blissful consciousness; Paramānanda-lahari, the wave of supreme bliss; or Satchidānanda, absolute existence, consciousness, and bliss.

21. Siddha Yoga regards the philosophical system of Kashmir Shaivism with the highest respect because it makes no distinctions of caste, color, or nationality. It is open to all.

22. The Self manifests in the form of *aham*, "I," and as material objects in the form of *idam*, "this." Siddha Yoga calls these the perceiver and the perceived.

23. Siddha Yoga reveres the world and takes delight in its evolution. It creates enjoyment of one's household duties and excites interest in one's lifework.

---

1. The powers of speaking, grasping, locomotion, excretion, and procreation. Also called organs of action.

24. Siddha Yoga respects marriage and does not condemn disciplined pleasure.

25. Siddha Yoga avoids all intoxicants, including marijuana, opium, cocaine, hashish, and other drugs. They corrupt the mind, destroy the intellect, and trouble one's life.

26. Siddha Yoga brings discipline to one's life and strengthens the body through meditation. It brings joy to the heart and makes the eyes sparkle with rays of love.

27. Siddha Yoga exists because of the Siddhas. It makes one swim in the ecstasy of the inner Self.

28. Siddha Yoga highly respects the sacred vows of all monks, *sannyāsins*,[2] and other great souls who have renounced everything. It respects the fact that they perform actions in the world in a detached manner while seeing Shiva everywhere.

29. Siddha Yoga does not engage in arguments or debates about acceptance and rejection. When there is nothing different from Shiva, what can be accepted or rejected? Siddha Yoga upholds equality.

30. Siddha Yoga considers all castes, religions, and sects to be its own and loves everyone with an open heart.

31. Siddha Yoga does not discriminate between men and wo-men, for the One who has become man has also become

---

2. Indian monks.

woman. The one Paramashiva has become two for the purpose of universal sport.

32. Siddha Yoga reveres the mother and the father. It honors the Guru and respects all people. Siddha Yoga encourages all the members of a family to live together with respect.

33. Arise and go to bed punctually. Eat and drink at a regular time. Speak in a disciplined manner. Always keep watch over your mind. A pure mind is the means of attaining divinity. This is the teaching of Siddha Yoga.

34. One creates one's own pain and pleasure. Therefore, one should be vigilant about one's actions. This is the wisdom of the Siddhas.

35. It is not a sin to lead a family life or to create children. Nor is it a sin to observe vows and discipline, or to earn money in an honorable way. The only sin is to insult one's own Self.

36. Never hate any religion, for all religions are equal. Never hate any castes, for Shiva exists in them all. Never hate the color of a person's skin, for the same Consciousness dwells in all colors. This is the wisdom of the Siddhas.

37. Sleep is the same for all people no matter what religion they pursue. Similarly, meditation on the Self is the same for all. Never doubt this. This is the wisdom of the Siddhas.

38. The heart of Siddha Yoga is meditation on one's own Self. Meditate daily on the inner Self according to your capacity. Do it at the same time every day for an hour or an hour and a half.

39. It is good to find a separate place for meditation. You should have a separate set of clothing and a warm blanket. It is also helpful to use incense and other fragrances. All these things are a part of the technique of Siddha Yoga.

40. Never deceive others by teaching yoga and meditation when you yourself do not know, contemplate, or practice them. To do this is to deceive the Self and to commit a sin.

41. A truly great person completes his *sādhanā*, or spiritual journey. That is his nature. It is also the way of the Siddha Path.

42. It is foolish for one to abandon spiritual practice if one does not meet with immediate success. Siddha Yoga teaches that failure can be a great instrument in the process of evolution.

43. Siddha Yoga does not accept the idea that something is impossible. It declares that there is nothing in the world which is impossible. Bhagīratha brought down the Ganges from heaven to earth, and it is still flowing today.[3]

44. When the inward-turned and thought-free mind meditates on the Self, love manifests. This is the wisdom of the Siddhas.

45. The Supreme Being dwells in the space of the inner heart. Remember this. This is the teaching of Siddha Yoga.

46. If greed lurks in the heart, that is vice enough for anyone. If one criticizes others, that is sin enough for anyone. But if

---

3. According to legend, the great King Bhagīratha managed to divert the holy river Ganges from heaven to earth. This almost impossible achievement has benefited India to this day.

the mind is pure, how can God be far away? If one possesses
virtue, what other qualities does one need? If one has attained Siddha Yoga, of what use are other spiritual practices?

47.   It is people who constitute a nation, and spreading the
teaching of the equality of all people makes a nation progress. The Siddha Path endeavors to spread this equality-
awareness.

48.   Siddha Yoga regards the wicked with compassion, for their
future is dark. Because of their attitude toward others, they
burn within and are reduced to ashes. This fire of negativity
is their only enemy, and it pursues them relentlessly. Therefore, take pity on them.

49.   Siddha Yoga teaches: "Without love, compassion, and
peace of mind, a person can never become happy. Without
love, even heaven is hell."

50.   People say, "Love your friends and hate your enemies." But
Siddha Yoga says, "Take pity on your enemies; bless those
who abuse and hate you; pray to the Lord for those who hurt
you." Then see what delight will be yours. God will come
looking for you.

51.   If you want love, love all. Respect everyone. Recognize
your loving Self in all. This is why in Siddha Yoga we say
every day with love and respect, "Welcome to all."

2

Kundalinī and Shaktipāt

52. The principal deity of Siddha Yoga is the great Kundalinī Shakti, who is also known as Chiti or Supreme Consciousness. She has assumed the form of the entire universe.

53. Kundalinī has three specific locations: at the base of the spine, in the heart, and at the crown of the head. She is awakened at the base of the spine and is also activated in the heart, where She manifests as bliss.

54. The creation that we see around us is the visible form of the universal Kundalinī. That conscious Kundalinī energy is known as the world.

55. Kundalinī is regarded as the highest deity. This great Shakti is supremely independent and has limitless power. She becomes the world and then sustains it. At the same time, She remains apart from it. Not only does She manifest in the form of the universe, but She also reabsorbs all manifested objects into Herself. This is the experience of Siddha Yoga.

56.   Because the great Shakti Kundalinī is a mighty power, She is free to perform any action. She brings into existence the entire creation, both seen and unseen. Siddha Yoga has complete understanding of this.

57.   Through Her mere thought, the mighty pulsating power of Kundalinī can bring into existence even objects which have never been seen. Siddha Yoga states that She could create a flower in the sky, make a barren woman give birth to a son, or manifest horns on a hare.

58.   She places limitations on space, time, and objects; but She Herself, being all-pervasive and eternal, is not bound by them. She is supremely pure and untouched. For that reason, She is known as Siddha Yoginī.

59.   Of her own free will, Shakti manifests in this world in the form of the knower, the known, and the process of knowing. She is all things both within and without, yet She exists apart from them all. This is why Siddha Yoga declares that She is of the nature of the Absolute.

60.   When we speak of Mahā Shakti, Parāsattā Chiti, Mātrikā, Gaurī, Lakshmī, Saraswatī,[4] and so on, we are actually referring to that Supreme Shakti Kundalinī who is the primordial seed of the universe. Although in reality this Shakti is only one, when She expands She overflows into innumerable currents. All the objects of the universe are Her forms. This is the perfect knowledge of the Siddhas.

---

4. Names of the universal creative energy.

61. This Supreme Shakti is not different from all existing things. Her independent power has become fivefold: Her power to give rise to bliss is *ānanda shakti*; Her power of creative will is *icchā shakti*; Her power to illumine is *chit shakti*; Her power to understand is *jnāna shakti*; and Her power to manifest all forms is *kriyā shakti*. It is *kriyā shakti* which, through *shaktipāt*, makes a seeker perform various kinds of yogic movements. This is the authentic experience of Siddha Yoga.

62. It is certain that the entire visible universe is the expansion of the sovereign power of the mighty Kundalinī. Although She exists in many forms, the independent Kundalinī Shakti vibrates without ceasing, primarily as *icchā, jnāna,* and *kriyā*. She carries out Her work in all beings, whether ignorant or wise. Seeing Her in all, Siddha yogis become overjoyed.

63. A person's desires exist in an unmanifest form in his subconscious mind. The Kundalinī Shakti knows them through Her power of knowledge and manifests them through Her power of action. Siddha yogis regard this mysterious and extraordinary Kundalinī as their beloved deity.

64. Kundalinī is a great spiritual power which cannot be detected with mechanical devices. For that reason, until now this has been a secret science. Whoever experiences it must do so with his own conscious body. He then tastes divine bliss and ecstasy. This is the secret of Siddha Yoga.

65. Western scientists have spent billions of dollars inventing machines in an attempt to gain knowledge of nature's subtle workings. They support their discoveries with mathematical calculations. Although their efforts are beneficial to many,

in order to experience Kundalinī Shakti one must use the instrument of the human body. One also needs the grace of the Guru and the compassion of Kundalinī. This is the statement of the Siddhas.

66. The conscious human body, which has been created by God, serves as the instrument as well as the laboratory. It is likely that the scientists of this age will investigate the laws of spiritual power just as they have investigated the laws of nature. That day is not far away. Siddha Yoga is the universal and all-pervasive Supreme Principle.

67. It is very important for a human being to awaken his Kundalinī. It is a power, a vibration, an extraordinary energy. It is the soul of an individual and his vital force. It is the conscious power behind the senses. It is that which inspires the intellect and makes the mind contemplate. Siddha Yoga teaches that this entire universe is pervaded by the great Shakti.

68. The individual soul dwells in the heart. In the heart, there are one hundred *nādīs*, or subtle channels. From each of these *nādīs*, one hundred other *nādīs* branch out. Seventy-two additional *nādīs* stem from each of these. And again, each of these *nādīs* has one thousand offshoots. In total, there are 720 million *nādīs* through which the particular *prāna*[5] known as *vyāna* circulates. Kundalinī, along with the *prāna*, pervades the body. Siddha Yoga accepts this statement from the *Prashnopanishad*.

---

5. Life force or vital energy. In the body, it takes five forms to perform five major functions: *prāna*, inhalation; *apāna*, exhalation; *vyāna*, pervasion; *udāna*, ascension; *samāna*, equalization.

69. Among all these *nādīs*, seventy-two thousand are important. Of these, one hundred are principal. And of these, three are particularly significant. Of these three, the most important is the *sushumnā*, which extends from the base of the spine to the crown of the head. The records of all the *karmas* of countless lifetimes are stored in the *sushumnā nādī.*

70. Shakti dwells at the base of the spine in the spiritual center called the *mūlādhāra*, and Shiva at the crown of the head in the center called the *sahasrāra*. The *sushumnā* extends from one to the other. The awakened Shakti rises from the base of the spine and unites with Shiva.[6] This union brings perfection. The state of Siddhahood arises from this.

71. *Shaktipāt*, or the awakening of Kundalinī, can occur in many different ways — through chanting, meditation, mantra repetition, Hatha Yoga postures, *bandhas*, *mudrās*, and other practices. Using these methods, a seeker has to struggle a great deal, and sometimes the results may be dangerous. Siddha yogis have the experience that it is easier to awaken the Shakti through the Guru's grace. This method is completely beneficial.

72. The initiation performed by the Guru takes place easily and simply. The Siddhas state that when the Guru sows the seed of Shakti, the seed develops very naturally into a tree with flowers and fruit.

73. In *shaktipāt*, the Shakti flows from one person to another either with or without the physical touch. The Shakti flows through the *nādīs* inside the body. When *shaktipāt* takes

---

6. The all-pervasive Supreme Consciousness or Ultimate Reality.

place, the Shakti permeates the entire body, creating a sensation similar to the heat of fire. This is experienced in Siddha Yoga.

74. Because the Shakti is subtler than the subtlest, some people may not be aware of it during the initial stages of practice. Others experience it immediately. Some perceive it as a flash of lightning. This light can be seen moving inside as well as outside the body. This is the experience of Siddha students.

75. A seeker also experiences the fact that the Shakti can be drawn into the body from different sources, such as the sun, clouds, fire, lightning, air, and ether. All objects are suffused with God's power. After the inner Shakti is awakened, a yogi through his will can draw the Shakti into his body from outside. That Shakti enters him and functions consciously. This is the experience of the Siddhas.

76. Unless the Kundalinī is awakened, a human being cannot evolve. Everyone is entitled to this — a child, an elderly person, a man, and a woman. The great Kundalinī Shakti exists equally in all, so Siddha Yoga considers everyone fit for its awakening.

77. The awakening of the Kundalinī is called initiation. It happens specifically at three different levels: *āṇavī, shakti,* and *shāmbhavī.*[7] It can occur through look, speech, or touch. In Siddha Yoga, the Guru can give initiation by staring fixedly at another person, by uttering the great mantra into his ear, or by touching him with the hand.

---

7. Three levels of initiation by the Guru, depending on the evolvement of the seeker. *Āṇavī* is initiation into mechanical and ritualistic practices. *Shakti* is initiation into subtle and psychological practices. *Shāmbhavī* is direct transmission of the state of Shiva, or Self-realization.

78. Through the will of the Guru, *shaktipāt* can also be given mentally. *Shaktipāt* can occur through the will of one who desires to give it. The one who wishes to receive Shakti should have love, devotion, steadfast faith in the Self, and the desire to attain it. This is the law of Siddha Yoga.

79. When *shaktipāt* takes place, some people experience it instantly in the form of visions of light, heaviness of the body, intoxication, bodily tremors, sweating, shivers of joy, and so on. These are the first signs of Siddha Yoga.

80. When the Shakti is awakened, various yogic movements take place. A person may utter different sounds. He may experience ecstasy, agitation, negativity, apathy, fear, loss of faith, and other feelings. These can happen in the initial stage of Siddha Yoga.

81. According to a person's temperament, he may receive *shaktipāt* in any one of twenty-seven different strengths. This is the teaching of Kashmir Shaivism. How a person receives it depends on his past actions, the actions that he is performing in this body, and his tendencies. This is the statement of the Siddhas.

82. Following *shaktipāt*, not everyone experiences the same *kriyās*. But though the *kriyās* may differ due to people's temperaments, the final experience is the same for everyone. There is only one experience of perfection. This is the conviction of all the Siddhas.

83.   In a human being, there are four bodies, one within the other: physical, subtle, causal, and supracausal.[8] As the Shakti works in all four bodies, She gives rise to various amazing experiences. This is the knowledge of the Siddhas.

84.   It is a philosophical premise that the microcosm is identical to the macrocosm. The great Shakti, the mother of the world, lives in the body as the microcosm. The entire universe exists in the seed of the heart, the inner Self.

85.   In the heart, there is a sublime and miraculous center. When the work of the Kundalinī begins there through the grace of a Siddha, a person can perceive distant objects and sounds. He acquires the knowledge of higher planes, of past lives, and of others' minds.

86.   Initiation, or Kundalinī awakening, gives a person complete knowledge. In the final stage of meditation, the awareness of So'ham[9] and "I am perfect" arises spontaneously within. It happens because the awakened Shakti is the embodiment of perfect knowledge. This is the indisputable experience of the Siddhas.

87.   A simple and powerful means of deepening meditation is to focus the mind on those great beings who are beyond attachment. Then meditation progresses very quickly. This is the remarkable effect of remembering the Siddhas.

---

8.   The physical body is experienced in the waking state. The subtle body (which includes mind, senses, and other subtle instruments) is the vehicle for the dream state. The causal body is experienced in deep sleep as blissful nonawareness. The supracausal body is made of pure Consciousness; it is the body of transcendental experience.

9.   Literally, "I am He" or "I am That."

88. There is no doubt that the sublime and divine Shakti dwells in every human being. Even if one cannot meditate deeply on one's own, by receiving Shakti from the Guru one will automatically experience all yogic *kriyās*. This is the wisdom of the Siddhas.

89. The mighty Kundalinī Shakti is the vital force. As fire, She gives heat; as the sun, She gives light; as rain, She brings showers; as wind, She blows everywhere. She is the earth. She exists in the form of all material objects.

90. No words can describe Her. She is a woman; She is a man. She is everything in the world. She is that which exists and that which does not exist.

3

The Inner Experience

91. Keep searching within. Plunge deeper and deeper to the realm of the heart. See the blissful effulgence there, beautiful and shimmering in various unique colors. Within the heart, in the space where the inhalation merges, perceive the thought-free state of love. Watch the play of the *mātrikā shakti*, the subtle vibrations that arise as thoughts and feelings and then subside back into the space of the heart. Then you will know that Siddha Yoga is within you.

92. Keep observing carefully where the inner fivefold actions[10] continue to arise and where they dissolve. Keep watching the petals of the heart lotus; observe how desire, greed, delusion, jealousy, enmity, arrogance, and envy form and dissolve in each petal. Where do they arise and subside? Why does this happen? Siddha Yoga concentrates on this inner understanding.

---

10. Activity of the individual's thoughts as they are created, sustained, dissolved, concealed in a seed form (stored as memory), or totally annihilated. Kashmir Shaivism teaches that this process parallels the cosmic process of creation, sustenance, etc.

93. Have you discovered where the inhalation goes when it merges in the heart? Who expels it in the form of the exhalation? Where does it merge outside? Who draws it in again? Siddha Yoga guides your attention to that.

94. Notice where the waves of feeling arise in the heart. Where does this infinite inner creation dissolve? Watch the miracle of the ever-new waves of this vast creation. These waves perpetually arise and subside. Siddha Yoga focuses your attention on this.

95. You have seen movies, disco, rock-and-roll, different resorts, clubs, fancy hotels, and parties. These things are alright; they are simply the products of the Shakti of those who are interested in them. But you have not seen where your awareness goes during deep sleep or through whose instigation you awaken. O friend, Siddha Yoga compels you to see that.

96. Observe something else with subtle understanding. Although you are asleep, who is awake within? That witness takes no rest and is inseparably one with your life. While remaining different from you, That watches everything which happens in your waking state as though it were a dream. Siddha Yoga inspires you to see That.

97. Plunge a little deeper. After seeing the infinite miracles of the heart, enter the supracausal body. Behold the vast center which is thought-free, blissful, and effulgent. How intriguing and beautiful it is, how perfectly smooth and even. In that space, there is light and nothing but light. Siddha Yoga calls it the bliss of *turīya*, the transcendental state.

98. Keep observing. As you continue to watch, the seer disappears. For a few seconds your existence is erased, just as a

grain of salt dissolves and becomes water. But have no fear — on reaching that state, you become eternally serene and unmoved. Then there is nothing but boundless ecstasy. Know that the Siddhas live there.

99.   That is the ocean of love. Like a wave, you drown in the ocean of bliss and become the ocean. Again and again, you arise and subside like a bubble in the ocean of love. Ah, what ecstasy! Ah, what sublime and exquisite bliss! What perfect peace and love! What independent contentment! That is the abode of the Siddhas.

100.   That is the center of the ecstatic beings. Its love is the true life. The individual derives his existence from it. The entire world dissolves in the ocean of love, then arises from it once again. That is the dwelling place of the ecstatic beings. If you seek the Siddhas, know that you will find them there.

101.   After entering within, slowly go higher. Slowly — there is no need to hurry. As you rise higher, rest a while in the space between the eyebrows. That is the passport office of the Guru. With love, devotion, and humility, get your visa there. Look: If you have any ego, throw it away like a worn-out shoe. Otherwise, this visa will be very difficult for you to obtain. Only through the grace of the Siddhas can it be acquired.

102.   After obtaining your visa, slowly and carefully proceed further. You will reach the divine world of the *sahasrāra*, which is composed of one thousand centers, each more sublime than the last. It is enchanting and infinitely beautiful. Each center embodies a different kind of understanding and knowledge. Siddha students have a picnic there.

103. In the vast, exquisite space of the *sahasrāra*, you will see the divine effulgence of a thousand blazing suns. Its beauty is utterly enchanting. This cool, divine light creates no heat. In it there are neither moon nor stars. This divine effulgence is the perfect image of supreme bliss. This is the statement of the great Siddhas.

104. In the *sahasrāra*, there is no heat of either fire or the sun. There is no coolness of the moon. Neither pain nor death can reach there. It is eternally suffused with bliss. Reaching there, yogis merge with that bliss. It is their true abode. Siddha Yoga affirms this.

105. It is also called the space of wisdom. It manipulates the entire body and is the center of all the *nādīs*. The yogic scriptures compare it to a thousand-petaled lotus. The center of that lotus is the abode of Lord Shiva. When Siddha yogis reach that space, they obtain undying awareness of Shiva.

106. In the center of the *sahasrāra* is the Blue Pearl, an exquisite, tiny blue light. Its effulgence is enchanting. Ah, who can describe its beauty? How can one understand its divinity? Although it is just a dot, this tiny light contains the entire universe. It is the form of the Supreme within us. The Siddhas call it the seed of the heart.

107. A yogi's meditation stabilizes in it. When he sees it, his entire body grows cold, his mind becomes silent, and for a few moments the movement of his vital force ceases. He loses himself in meditation.

108. When the Supreme Lord within becomes pleased with a yogi, the Guru's compassionate glance descends on him. At

that time, the Blue Pearl emerges from his eyes and manifests before him. As it stands before him, his good fortune blossoms. The Blue Pearl expands and permeates the entire cosmos. Having the vision of its pervasion of the universe, a yogi becomes worthy of the title Siddha.

109.   Compared to the expansion of the Blue Pearl, the universe appears to be as tiny as a dot. When the Blue Pearl expands in this way, an extraordinary Blue Being manifests from its center. He has a form of the utmost beauty, but it is not composed of the gross elements. Tukārām Mahārāj, a Siddha, said, "That form is the embodiment of Consciousness." The Siddhas proclaim that the Blue Lord pervades all three worlds.

110.   That being, the embodiment of Consciousness, is made of extraordinary light — blue, red, and all the colors of the morning sun. He is a miraculous, radiant being. In meditation, He stands directly before the yogi. There are no words to describe His beauty. Jnānadeva, a supreme Guru among Siddhas, called Him the light of Consciousness.

111.   The Blue Being is the radiance of the perfect knowledge of divine realization. A vision of Him is considered to be the realization of the form of God. Although the Blue Being has a form, He is actually formless. This is the experience of the Siddhas.

112.   He has created the universe, pervaded it, and assumed its form. He stands quietly for several seconds before a lover of the Guru. He walks around the meditating yogi and utters a few words. These words brim with sweetness and mystery. At this point, the yogi is very near the state of Siddhahood.

113.   The mighty One, the Blue Lord, the Sovereign of Consciousness, stands before the yogi who has received the Guru's grace and utters these words: "I have eyes in all My limbs. I can see every atom of the universe. All My limbs — My hands, legs, and head — as well as every pore of My body can speak." In this way, He addresses the Siddha yogi for a few moments.

114.   That which Kashmir Shaivism refers to as the Supreme Pulsation, Consciousness, or the mighty Shakti is the one who utters these secret words. Just as Consciousness expands, pervades the entire universe, and once again contracts, similarly, the Blue Being, Consciousness, the Great Light once again becomes the Blue Pearl, as tiny as a sesame seed, and re-enters the body through the eyes. It lives eternally in the *sahasrāra*. The great Kundalinī yogi now becomes established in the seat of Siddhahood.

115.   At this point, the yogi's understanding changes and he is totally transformed. With his own eyes, he fully perceives the Truth. As he ponders his realization again and again, his hair stands on end, his eyes brim with tears, sweat pours from him, and his body trembles. Becoming ecstatic and intoxicated with love, he is firmly established in Siddhahood.

116.   Then he spontaneously obtains complete knowledge of the formless. Just as in the state of ignorance he used to say, "I am the body," now he very naturally knows, "I am perfect." As a matter of course, he experiences perfection everywhere. He is filled with love. He considers the world to be the expansion of his own Self. He is aware that he is in the world and the world is in him. He experiences oneness. This is the perfect attainment of the Siddha yogi.

4

Nityānanda

117.   After the realization of the form of God, the yogi naturally becomes established in formlessness. Wherever he may go, he finds only his Self. He does not have to become angry with the world. He neither scoffs at worldly pleasures, nor takes any interest in them. For him, the world is entertainment, like watching a movie.

118.   After realization, some beings remain ecstatic. They live in our world, but no matter where or in what condition they are, the world appears differently to them than it does to us. For them, the world has become heaven because they see it in the divine light of Consciousness. "The world is as you see it"[11] — this is the wisdom of the Siddhas.

119.   Siddhas are supremely independent. They are totally immersed in God at all times. Their state and behavior are strange. Some look outwardly foolish although they are inwardly intelligent. Others are scholarly and give birth to the literature of Truth. Some appear to be crazy. This is the way of the Siddhas.

---

11. The philosophy of the sage Vasishtha as expressed in *Yoga Vasishtha.*

120. Even though some live like kings, they are flawless in renunciation, discrimination, and detachment. They are free of expectations. Although they live like kings, their Siddhahood is perfect. Their position is due to fortune and destiny. It is given by God.

121. O my Bhagawān Nityānanda, you were a great renunciant. Although countless objects used to lie around you, you neither touched them with your hands nor even cast your eyes on them. You lived in a solitary place, in a jungle where once there was not even a means of access. Now, it has become a shrine. This is the destiny of Siddhas.

122. O Bhagawān Nityānanda, you were a supreme *avadhūta*.[12] You wore only a loincloth, but you were born a Siddha. In your younger days, you served a great ascetic, just as Shrī Krishna, who was the Absolute made manifest, spent some time serving Sāndīpani. The great beings do such things in order to teach people. This is the wisdom of the Siddhas.

123. O Nityānanda, you were the crown jewel of all *avadhūtas*. You knew the past, present, and future. Even if you spoke only one word, it never went to waste. You were the image of renunciation. You were always utterly ecstatic within yourself. To remain ecstatic within is the state of the Siddhas.

124. O Nityānanda, you were perpetually bathed in bliss. Your name itself was bliss. When you laughed, joy and ecstasy burst forth from every pore of your body, as if your skin ripped open with the sudden outrush of your joy. You always spoke

---

12. A realized being who remains above body-consciousness.

aphoristically. Although you might utter one brief word, it would contain as much meaning as a lengthy discourse. Sometimes you would remain silent for two or three days at a time. This is the extraordinary way of the Siddhas.

125.   O Nityānanda, Lord of *avadhūtas*, you had a dark body. Your belly was enlarged by the spontaneous retention of your breath.[13] Although your eyes looked outward, your gaze was directed within. Your eyes were half-closed and shone like the morning sun. A smile always played upon your lips. Your hands were large and generous. When you walked, your gait was like that of an intoxicated elephant. You were a Siddha who stole everyone's mind.

126.   Sometimes when you closed your eyes, it would take you an hour or two to open them. Enjoying the natural state of a Siddha, at times you would sleep for hours on end, immersed in the ecstasy of your own Self. Although thousands of people came to see you, there was no noise; the atmosphere was hushed. You did not have to give lectures. Merely by seeing you, people would be consoled. You were the Lord of Siddhas.

127.   O Nityānanda, you used to say, "The Self is the Supreme Truth. There is nothing more sublime than the Self. Hey! The Self is within. Turn within." In this way, you taught with just a few words. For you, within and without were the same. You always dwelled within. What a great Siddha you were!

---

13. A yogic practice called *kumbhaka*, performed for achieving a thought-free state of mind. In its spontaneous manifestation as described here, it implies prolonged absorption in the thought-free state and the retention of great power in the yogi.

128. O Nityānanda, your words were mantras; your speech was scripture. Your behavior embodied the teachings of yoga. The place where you lived was immaculate; it always looked freshly scrubbed no matter how many thousands of people came to see you.

129. O Shrī Gurudev, in you one could see that the sublime *shaivī khecharī mudrā* of Shaivism had taken up residence. Lord Shiva described this *shaivī mudrā*, this pure *khecharī* which is the state of Shiva. He said that the eyes remain fixed and unblinking but see nothing. Although they appear to look outward, the gaze is directed within. The mind is quiet, not dwelling on any thought, and the vital force is still but not forcibly retained. O Nityānanda, you lived in this sublime *mudrā* of the Siddhas.

130. The human body is made of seven components,[14] but in a Siddha these elements have been consumed in the fire of Kundalinī meditation. A new *rasa*, or bodily fluid, has been created. It is the embodiment of Consciousness and bliss. Because of it, the body of a Siddha is suffused with the sweetness of love.

131. The sublime sweetness of Kundalinī plays throughout the entire body of a great being. In ecstasy, he is one with the perfect bliss of the Absolute. In his company, people naturally experience joy. O Nityānanda, thousands of people sat in silence before you. Everyone was intoxicated. Wherever a great Siddha dwells, the atmosphere is permeated with serenity and love.

---

14. Lymphatic fluid, blood, flesh, fat, bone, marrow, and sexual fluid.

132.   O Gurudev, you are still at work even though you are no longer in your physical body. In your inner, conscious body, you appear to many people. I have received numerous letters from individuals saying, "Nityānanda Bābā told me this or that." Siddhahood is ancient, eternal, and true.

133.   O Bhagawān Nityānanda, you are everywhere; I have utter faith in this. O my Gurudev, you are in the light of the sun, in the coolness of the moon, in the gusts of wind. In the heavens, you shine as the twinkling of the stars. O great Siddha Nityānanda, with devotion, complete knowledge, and understanding, one can see that you are manifest even though you appear to be concealed.

134.   Human beings suffer only because they lack understanding. The great being Ekanāth spoke from the highest level of understanding when he said, "I will lead my life with great joy. I will fill all three worlds with bliss." O Nityānanda, you fill the entire universe. As another Siddha yogi, Vasuguptāchārya, said, "The pulsation of the cosmos is the mighty Shakti of the Guru."

135.   With firm understanding and truthfulness, I say, "O Nityānanda, you are before me, behind me, on either side of me, and below me. It is you who gives and you who receives." Vasugupta said that the world is a play of Consciousness. The world is a play of the essence of Nityānanda.

136.   The great saint Jnāneshwar Mahārāj said, "O Gurunāth, when you conceal yourself from someone, he sees this world as full of various strange and separate things. But when you reveal yourself, you and you alone remain. The world ceases to exist for him." In the same way, O Shrī Guru Nityānanda, when a person forgets you, he perceives the play of the world.

When he remembers you, the world becomes the embodiment of you. This is the statement of the Siddhas.

137.   O man, give up the weakness of your delusion and sense of duality. Make your heart pure. Enter completely within and see that it is Nityānanda who pervades the world. Vasugupta asked, "What place or object lacks Consciousness?" What time is there without Nityānanda?

138.   O friend, improve yourself. Purify yourself. In the fire of meditation, wash the dirt from the mirror of your intellect. Sadguru Nityānanda dwells in a pure heart and a clean mind. This is the wisdom of the Siddhas.

139.   How can you forget the Truth? Why do you value false-hood so highly and then pay the price you yourself have created? Open your eyes. Whatever you may do, do it for your inner Nityānanda. Become alert. Change the prescription of your glasses. Then look and you will see only Nityānanda. This is what the Siddha yogis have told you. This is the teaching of Siddha Yoga.

5

The Lords of Equality

140. These days in the spiritual field, there are many writers, lecturers, so-called great beings, and people who call themselves God. There are people who claim to be Siddhas, yet change their names again and again. It is very likely that some bound souls are hiding among the Siddhas. Their ageless ignorance gives rise to jealousy, and this in turn creates duality and the desire to see others' faults. But a true Siddha avoids such destructive action.

141. Someone once wrote in an article, "Muktānanda is not yet perfect." I said, "That's fine. Perhaps I have had wrong understanding of myself and he is very kindly pointing it out to me. But one thing surprises me. Where did he get the meter to determine this?" Bhagawān Nityānanda never liked to criticize any religion, sect, or person. If anyone found fault with someone else, he would say, "Hey! You have faulty vision. Rām is in all." This is the sign of a supreme Siddha.

142. In the great Indian epic, the *Mahābhārata*, a dialogue takes place between two people, one evil and one good. Lord Krishna asks the virtuous Dharmarāya, "Can you point out a

sinner or a wicked person in this crowd?" Dharmarāya re-
plies, "No, no! Here there are only good people." Then
Krishna asks the wicked Duryodhana, "Can you point out a
good person in this gathering?" Duryodhana says, "They're
all sinners. There is not a single good person here." So you
see, one's vision creates one's world. To a Siddha's vision, all
are equal. A Siddha has risen above criticizing others.

143.   In the *Yoga Vāsishtha*, it is said, "The world is as you see it."
You create your own experience according to your perception. A Siddha sees the world according to his own vision,
and a bound person does the same. Kashmir Shaivism says
that all beings are equal. Equal vision is the means of attaining Siddhahood.

144.   Suppose that the question were asked, "What is the meaning of *da*?" One person might say, "*Da* means *dambha*,
pretension." A second person might say, "*Da* means *dāridrya*,
poverty of understanding." A third might say, "*Da* means *da
da*, the way a farmer calls a bull; so *da* might refer to a bull."
These people's interpretations would indicate their capacity
and attainment. But God's loving look permeates the eyes of
Siddhas, so they see only good even in defects.

145.   Many are the ways of Siddhas. I knew a great Siddha,
Zipruannā, who was always naked. He would lie on a heap of
garbage. He ate whatever passersby gave him. Although he
sat surrounded by filth, he was never affected by it. He saw
only equality everywhere. He was always happy. Although
he was in the body, he knew that he was totally different
from it. He was an ecstatic Siddha.

146.   Zipruannā was omniscient. He had full knowledge of both
past and future. He spoke in the Marāthi language, and his

speech was simple and straightforward. In his village, he always roamed wherever and whenever he liked. If anyone spoke to him, he would reply with only a few words. He was always ecstatic within himself. There were a large number of Hindus and Moslems in his village, and both groups respected him greatly. One has to be supremely fortunate to meet such a Siddha.

147. There was another great being called Ranga Avadhūt, whom I used to visit now and then. He was a great scholar and came to our Āshram twice. He lived on the banks of the holy Narmadā River and would bathe three times each day. He always traveled on foot. He would never sit in a car, but occasionally he would ride in a horse carriage. He was a great Siddha.

148. People used to look upon Ranga Avadhūt as a divine incarnation. He wore a loincloth and often carried a long stick. He ate simple, light food. He spoke very little and in plain, straightforward language. He was so completely free of pride and ego that he had become love incarnate. He used to meet people punctually. He listened to others' questions about their pains and pleasures and gave them advice. I loved him very much. He was such a great Siddha that people considered him the incarnation of Guru Dattātreya.[15]

149. I met another saint called Ranchod Bāpuji, who also visited our Āshram once. He did a great deal of work among the needy. Wherever there was famine, he would rush to assist the starving villagers by giving them food, water, and clothing. He was also a great Siddha.

---

15. An incarnation of Brahmā, Vishnu, and Rudra, the Hindu trinity of creation, sustenance, and destruction, combined in one form.

150. Bāpuji was omniscient. He, too, ate very simple, light food. He was a great renunciant and very loving and powerful. He removed the pain and poverty of many. Enormous crowds of thousands of people used to gather around him. Sometimes he would disappear for days on end, and no one would know where he had gone. Suddenly he would reappear in the midst of the people. His behavior was extraordinary. He was incomparably secretive. It is impossible to truly describe him. Such rare Siddhas occasionally manifest in the world.

151. Siddhārūdha was another great being. He lived in Hūbli, a large city in south India. All who came to him were given food. No one remained hungry. Then, as well as now, his entire āshram continually reverberated with the chanting of *Om Namah Shivāya*. People used to consider him the incarnation of Shiva. He was one of the great Siddhas.

152. In Siddhārūdha's āshram, *satsang* was held both in the morning and in the evening. Scriptural discussions were always going on. Great scholars and philosophers lived there and received Siddhārūdha's grace. In fact, all the religious people of the area used to gather there. They referred to his abode as Kailāsa.[16] Even a fortunate person only rarely sees such a great Siddha.

153. There was another saint called Hari Giri Bābā. I spent a good deal of time with him, too. He lived like a gentleman. He wore a turban of expensive silk with a gold border, an elegant coat, and costly shoes. He always roamed here and there, even at night. If anyone invited him for a meal, he

16. Heavenly abode of Lord Shiva.

would eat and then leave. His state was exceedingly strange. He talked to himself, and his speech was odd. He was also a great Siddha yogi.

154. Most of the time, Hari Giri wandered around a dry river bed. He would select tiny pebbles, talk to them, and stuff his pockets with them. Sometimes he would gaze off into the distance and scold. Occasionally he would talk to the wind. His was a curious state. Whenever I went through difficult times during my *sādhanā*, he would visit me. He would help me understand something and then leave immediately. He was a Siddha who knew the past, present, and future.

155. Sāi Bābā of Shirdi was also great. He satisfied his hunger with the alms he received daily. He was fond of listening to music. At any time, he could give people fistfuls of money from his empty pockets. He wore a long, plain robe and a scarf around his head. He was a great Siddha.

156. Sāi Bābā was worshipped by everyone — the rich as well as the poor. If someone gave him a gift, he would give it to anyone who happened to be there. He had no desire for possessions. He was supremely compassionate and eased the pain and suffering of the poor. His influence is still felt throughout the world. People had absolute faith in his greatness. When he shed his body, he told people, "Now the stone of my *samādhi* shrine[17] will respond to you." Since then, Shirdi has become a magnificent and holy place. There is a constant stream of visitors from near and far. Facilities have been provided so that many people can stay there. It has become a great Siddha shrine.

---

17. Burial place of a great saint embodying his power.

157. Once again, I am reminded of Bhagawān Nityānanda. To remember him is more than enough for my small life. At least I knew him. What greater fortune than that could there be? Kabīr, the great poet-saint, said, "One fragrant *champā* blossom is better than a stack of dry grass." In the same way, the Siddhahood of Bhagawān Nityānanda was sufficient for me.

158. One day in Nityānanda's presence, I referred to someone as a crook. Immediately Gurudev said, "Hey, Muktānanda! Is there really any crooked person in this world? It is just the crookedness of your cleverness. Everything is the pervasion of the Supreme Truth. God has created the play of the world for His own pleasure. No one in the world is crooked." Ah, how perfect he was. What Siddhahood!

159. He continued, "O Muktānanda! You are seeing with petty understanding. With this kind of awareness, you are heading in the wrong direction. Change your outlook. Correct your understanding. Then see that the world is just a play, an entertaining movie. It is neither true nor false. Know this secret. Only then will you attain something." What a great teaching that was, and how absolutely true. What divine wisdom of the Self. This is the teaching of the compassionate Siddha Guru.

160. Nityānanda taught: "All religions belong to the One. All sects are formed for Him alone. Nevertheless, through their own inspiration, the people who found sects give many forms to that One. No matter how many ornaments one makes, they all come from the same gold." Gurudev's teachings were sublime and true. The Siddhas are the lords of equality.

161. Since I loved Shiva, I also loved to worship the Shiva *lingam*.[18] I had faith that if God exists in all, then the *lingam* must also be a perfect manifestation of Him. One day as I was returning from worshipping the *lingam*, Nityānanda asked me, "What were you doing?" I replied, "Bathing Rudra." Gurudev laughed and said, "The one you are worshipping is also within you. In fact, He gives you the power to do it. Worship Him through meditation. Meditation is worship; meditation is a ritual bath. Attain Him through meditation." What true understanding. He opened the gate of heaven for me. This is how the teachings of the Siddhas are.

162. I am reminded of Tulasidās, another great being, who said, "Keep the company of enlightened Gurus with great humility, with unaffected love, and without ego. Just as the sun dispels darkness, the Guru banishes ignorance." This is absolutely true. Without the aid of a Siddha, one cannot easily sail across the ocean of the world.

163. If a person with a taintless heart and a vigilant and pure mind keeps the company of a Siddha just for a moment, half a moment, or even half of that, he can instantly go across the ocean of mundane existence. How wonderful Gurudev's teachings were! His words were a lotion which removed blindness. Only by becoming a fish can one know how a fish lives. To understand a great being, one first has to become one with him. That is true knowledge.

164. My Gurudev spoke very seldom — sometimes every few hours, sometimes once a day, or once every several days. Occasionally he would speak only once every three months

---

18. A representation of the formless aspect of Shiva (Rudra) usually worshipped by ritualistic bathing of the image.

or every six months. Then again he might not speak for nine months at a time. However, when Nityānanda spoke even for ten minutes, it was more than enough for my entire life. I can now pass on his words to the whole world. A handful of the words of a Siddha contain great power and blaze with Shakti.

165. I do not attach much importance to the statements of people who say that they have become Siddhas without the grace of another Siddha, or that they are the highest God of all, or that they hold the loftiest position. These statements show that they have not yet reached that state. The gracious glance of a Siddha is priceless. I am alive because of it.

166. The entire creation as well as all philosophies and all knowledge are contained within Gurudev's glance. In his vision, the world is sustained as the world. I honor that gracious glance. It is sufficient for me. What joy, what ecstasy and love it contains! I embrace that ecstasy and immerse myself blissfully in the love of the Siddhas.

167. Let those with the tendency to differentiate measure what is high and what is low as if they were in a grocery store. I do not want that. My only desire is to experience Nityānanda's love in everyone, to experience equality everywhere, to become a true lover in order to taste again and again the love of my Gurudev, who is established in the awareness of the Self of all. May I bow my head before such Siddhas. May I offer my ego at the Siddhas' feet.

6

The City of Love

168. What is the state of an ecstatic being? To be happy within himself, to speak to his friends about this ecstasy, to open his heart to his companions about this knowledge with joy, peace, and love. O friend, selfish knowledge, or even the pursuit of Siddhahood and spirituality, are joyless *sādhanā* when love is missing. I do not want that. Love, happiness, and ecstasy dwell among the Siddhas.

169. Love is the supreme attainment. Without love, everything is useless. The world manifests through the power of God's love, it is sustained by love, and it will ultimately merge into love. That love throbs within us at all times. Siddha Yoga is the attainment of love. It is becoming anchored in love.

170. There is boundless love within. It is supremely true. We inhale and exhale because of its pulsation. The *prāna* circulates throughout the body due to the throb of love. It is love which has given the eyes the ability to perceive forms. This independent love is eternal bliss. It is the abode of the Siddhas.

171.   Through love in the form of fire, all that we eat and drink is digested in the stomach.[19] Through love, that digested food is converted to blood and distributed throughout the body. All the bodily functions are motivated by love. Love enraptures the Siddhas. It is their attainment.

172.   A human being cannot live without inner love. The Self is called *satchidananda* — absolute existence, consciousness, and bliss. It is the Supreme Truth. To attain love, we have to turn within. By doing this, we discover the vastness of love. The Siddhas dwell in this city of love.

173.   In the *Shrimad Bhagavatam*, there is a saying: "The real path is that which is trodden by the great beings." Love, that supreme and eternal bliss, was the path trodden by the great beings, sages, and souls who saw equality everywhere. It was through this path that they found the object of their search. Love is the seat of the Siddhas.

174.   The awareness of equality is the highest attainment. Human beings are troubled by duality and a sense of differences. Disparity exists because of delusion, anger, attachment, and ignorance. When we keep the company of great beings, duality turns into unity and disparity into equality. When we have this understanding, we become worthy of receiving the grace of a Siddha. Then we obtain the ocean of love.

175.   Nityananda had attained the supreme state. It was extraordinary. He lived in the ecstasy of natural *samadhi*.[20] He

---

19. According to yogic doctrine, the process of digestion takes place because of a "gastric fire."

20. The superconscious state of God-realization.

maintained that state at every moment. He was intoxicated with love. Wherever he went, he walked around God. The movements of his body were his worship of God. His sleep was the divine state of *samādhi*. He was absorbed in his own Self, and that absorption was the worship of all. The Siddhas' state is beyond mind and speech.

176.   Whatever Nityānanda said was equivalent to a Vedic mantra. For him, both a house and a desert were pleasant resting places. For him, eating and drinking were sublime acts of worship. He did not have to close his eyes, plug his ears, or practice any strenuous techniques. With his open eyes, he saw the true beauty of this world of forms.

177.   Because he was absorbed in his inner divinity, base desire could never approach him. Whether he was standing or sitting, his natural *samādhi* was never disturbed. Such was his state. This state is called *unmanī*, the state beyond the mind. It transcends the body, mind, and speech. How can one write about it? This supreme state transcends body-consciousness. Pain and pleasure cannot touch it. A Siddha, who is anchored in this state, has become one with his own Self. To compare such a Siddha with God is a small matter.

178.   Because Nityānanda was immersed in the ecstasy of inner love, he spoke little. There was no need for him to speak. If someone owns a jewel case full of diamonds, why should he have to open it again and again? If a swan reaches Mānasa Lake on Mount Kailāsa, why should it return to ordinary rivers and streams? When a person has become the all-pervasive Consciousness, why should he open his eyes and look outside? If a person watched Nityānanda with love

even for a few moments, he became like him. Very few
such Siddhas come into the world.

179.   In Pandharpur,[21] I met a great being called Bāpumāyī. He
would wake up in the morning and take about a four-mile
walk through Pandharpur. He used to wear a loincloth and
another small cloth to cover his body. He carried a bundle of
three sticks over his shoulder. When he walked down the
road, the shopkeepers would give him money. Within two
hours, his fists would be full of money. He would take it to the
graveyard where he lived. To him this place was a palace.

   Once I followed him. As he left the city on his way to the
graveyard, he suddenly looked back. "Why are you following
me?" he asked.

   I replied, "I want to come to your home."

   "Hey, you're a nice man," he said. "I belong to a low caste
and live in a graveyard. You shouldn't come with me."

   I insisted, "You are much better than I am. In my eyes,
you belong to the highest class. I want to go with you."

   He walked off and I followed him until we finally reached
the graveyard. The holy river Chandrabhāgā flows by that
place. He stood before the river and addressed it: "O Mother,
keep this money with you." He threw the money into the
water, saying, "I have no place to keep it. You take care of it."
Then he sat peacefully under a tree in the graveyard. I
prostrated fully before him, touched his feet, and sat down.

   He said, "I belong to a low caste. You are a *sannyāsin*,
Nārāyana Himself.[22] It's not good for you to commit the sin
of bowing to me."

---

21. In Mahārāshtra state; a place of pilgrimage.

22. When a *sannyāsin* renounces the pleasures of the earthly, ancestral, and
heavenly worlds, it is commonly considered that the merit earned by his action
raises him to the level of Nārāyana, or God.

I protested, "Bāpumāyīji, I know myself very well, and I know you, too. I have come here greedy for some real nourishment. If you would be less miserly, I would be more fortunate."

He said, "Go to the temple and see the statue of Vitthal."

"I've done all that," I replied. "Now I'm sitting right before the moving, speaking Vitthal."

"I feel that I am the lowest of all," he said. "Don't you feel ashamed being here with me?" Then he added softly, "O swāmi, everything is the embodiment of God. There is nothing else. The Lord is above, below, to the left and right. You are that God. There is nothing else but Him. Chant His name with great ecstasy. Now go."

I said, "Come with me to Yeola."

"No, no," he answered. "Why should I leave this heaven and go somewhere else?" By this time it was midnight. "Now leave. Wherever you go, I am with you. Go to your own heaven, Ganeshpuri." Then he said something else. I became ecstatic and slept in the graveyard. I had arrived in the town only that evening, and already I had met such a great Siddha.

180. There was another great being called Narasinga Swāmi who used to wander through the streets of the town of Pandharpur. He was not emaciated like Bāpumāyī. His body was so strong that even a wrestler seemed puny by comparison. Narasinga Swāmi went around naked. He would bathe wherever he found a water faucet. No one could count how many times he bathed during the day and night. He observed silence. If he spoke at all, he would say only one or two very mysterious words.

People would give him things with great love. As he walked down the street, he would enter a restaurant. Inside he would say, "Yes, yes," point out a number of items, and eat a large amount. Then he would leave and continue walking down the street. When he came across another water faucet, he would bathe again and then go into another restaurant.

This play would continue throughout the day. At night, he would lie down on the ground in front of any store, fall sound asleep, and begin to snore. The earth was his bed. The sky in all four directions was his blanket. How radiant, how joyful he was! He did not feel cold, nor did the earth give him discomfort. He was independent of his body.

I slept by his side one night. When he woke up at three o'clock in the morning, I also got up. He sang a poem in the Kannada language, the essence of which was: "What should one own, and what should one renounce? When both these notions have disappeared, what does a fully ripened yogi need? What does he reject?" By the time he had bathed, one of the restaurants had opened. He immediately went in and ate. Then he slowly began to walk down the road. I went up to him and bowed.

He said, "What I said is all there is." That was my meeting with this strange Siddha.

181. From there, I went to visit Adoni Lakshmībāi. She was an extraordinary yoginī who had attained an exalted state. Four women used to take care of her. If they dressed her, she would toss the clothes aside. Once she noticed a man coming to see her. She yelled, "Ah, that scoundrel is coming here! He's a cheat; he's greedy. He wants to please me by bringing bananas, sweets, and money. Even though he's had three wives, he has no children. He wants a son." Then she covered her head with a blanket and went to sleep.

When the man arrived, the women attendants asked him, "Did you bring bananas?"

"Yes," he replied.

"Have you had three wives?" they asked. He had. "Do you want a child?" He did. Then they said, "Now you can leave!"

The whole time the man was there, Adoni Lakshmībāi had remained asleep. The moment he left, she awoke. Nine months later, his wife gave birth to a son. What a unique Siddha yoginī! She was truly extraordinary.

182.   Many years ago in the town of Ālandi in Mahārāshtra, there lived a sublime Siddha yogi. His name was Jnāneshwar Mahārāj. Although he was young, he was very compassionate and considered everyone as equal. When any other Siddha came near him, Jnāneshwar always appeared to be just one inch greater.

He lived with his brothers and his younger sister Muktābāi. At that time, there was in their village a very orthodox priest called Visoba Khechar. Out of jealousy of the children's attainment, he had instructed the village shopkeepers not to sell anything to Jnāneshwar's family.

One day Muktābāi wanted to make *puranpoli*, a sweet bread, but when she went to the market, no one would sell her a pan. She returned home and called her brother Jnāneshwar. He said, "Don't worry, my sister. You can cook the bread on my back." He got down on his hands and knees, saying, "Inside, there is a mighty fire. Let it blaze." The moment he spoke these words, his inner fire was kindled through his yogic power and his back became red hot. Muktābāi cooked the bread on his back and fed everyone.

Jnāneshwar Mahārāj was such a great and powerful yogi that the eight great supernatural powers followed at his heels. Even today his writings are read and revered throughout the world.

183.   Muktābāi was a great yoginī even as a child. Like her brother Jnāneshwar, she was a great poet. One day her brother sent the famous yogi Shrī Changadev to see her. Arriving unexpectedly, he accidentally entered the room where Muktābāi was taking a bath.

As he was rushing from the room, Muktābāi shouted after him: "Fool! After all your years of study, you are still no yogi. You have seen so many naked cows grazing on the meadows. O Chāngadev, you should see me as you see those cows. Because you have not received the blessings of a perfect master, you are still not free from the duality of ego — men and women, high and low. Lose your ego and there will be no difference between you and me. Then you will realize your pure Self, which is beyond all these outer appearances."

Hearing these words, Shrī Chāngadev ran back into the room and fell prostrate before Muktābāi, calling her Mother over and over. With the last trace of his ego washed away, he became as pure and perfect as the rays of the sun.

Muktābāi was such a great and powerful Siddha yoginī that one word from her could transform a seeker.

184. In Pandharpur lived a saint called Janābāi who was a devotee of Nāmadev Mahārāj. Her heart and mind were pure. She was devoted to God and indifferent to the world. She was always absorbed in her work. She spent her life grinding grain, and as she did this, she constantly chanted God's name. Seeing her love and devotion, God would assume a form and, out of love for her, would help her grind the grain

This is what the Siddhas say about Janābāi, and I have complete faith in it. What is impossible for God?

185. The great Queen Mīrābāi is a well-known historical figure. She was a great lover of Krishna and became so immersed in devotion to God that she lost interest in her high position. If a person has swum in the ocean of love, why would she take interest in a river or stream? Mīrābāi used to wear anklets and chant and dance in the temple. Chanting is a great therapy. I do not know how far one can go with modern psychotherapy,

but I know that the therapy of chanting can wholly rejuvenate a person. Mīrābāi was one of the Siddha yoginīs. She was once given poison to drink. Chanting God's name, she drank it, considering it a blessing from God. It did not affect her. This shows the power of chanting.

186.   There was another yoginī named Sakhubāi. She was a householder. She loved the saints and the holy town of Pandharpur but had to live with her very strong willed mother-in-law.

One day Sakhubāi wanted to visit Pandharpur, but her mother-in-law refused to let her go. When Sakhubāi prepared to leave anyway, her mother-in-law tied her to a post.

God's power is so extraordinary that He can do and undo anything. Through His thought alone, the world comes into existence, so what can be impossible for Him?

Sakhubāi wept, saying, "O Lord, I've heard that you take care of your devotees. Can't this poor woman have the *darshan* of Pandharpur and your pilgrims there? Won't you have compassion on me?" The *Bhagavad Gītā* says that if we remember God even once, He remembers us a hundred times. At that point, God assumed a form identical to that of Sakhubāi, released her, and tied Himself to the post.

Sakhubāi immediately went to Pandharpur and met all the saints there. The Lord, who is dear to His devotees, had fulfilled her desires, and she returned promptly. God tied her to the post again and disappeared.

Meanwhile, the mother-in-law had gone to the river to fetch water. Some pilgrims happened to meet her there and said to her, "We saw your daughter-in-law in Pandharpur. She is on her way back; in fact, she must have arrived by now." The mother-in-law's eyes grew red with anger, and she rushed home. But when she arrived, she saw Sakhubāi still tied to the post. She questioned her, and Sakhubāi told the truth.

Everyone felt very sorry and said, "Oh! It was God Himself who took Sakhubāi's form. Our own blindness deceived us, and we didn't recognize Him." There is no doubt that a person reaps the fruits of his own actions. The great sage Nārada said that a genuine devotee always remains immersed in God. It is so true. God is wholly under the control of His devotees. Sakhubāi became a great Siddha yoginī even while leading the life of a householder.

187. Another great and very well-respected woman saint was Rabiā Bāsari. She was a renunciant who had attained perfect knowledge. She had led a just life, and even the eminent saint Hassan revered her. She had many miraculous powers. If she did not go to Mecca to see God, He would come to her. I have read about this. One day a mendicant was praying to God, "O Lord, open the door for me." Rabiā, who was also present, said, "O brother, when was God's door closed?" She was a remarkable Siddha yoginī who had attained God and who had discovered the secret of knowledge.

188. Akkamahādevi lived in Karnātaka. She was a great renunciant and was always absorbed in chanting the five-syllable mantra *Om Namah Shivāya*. She was the disciple of Shrī Basaveshwar, a Siddha who had attained the state of Shiva. Her great love forced God to manifest before her in the form of Mallikārjuna in the renowned holy place of Shrīshailam. Her poems were like divine mantras.

189. There have been countless other women saints and yoginīs. I could write forever about them. I will mention only a few of their names: Shivabhaktā, Lalleshwarī of Kashmir, Phooli-bāi, Jayadevi, Bahinābāi, Mallammā, Anasūyā, Gargi (the knower of the Absolute), and Maitreyī. In India, there have been many Siddha yoginīs to whom people pray every morning. I welcome them all with love.

7

The State of a Siddha

190.   O Shrī Gurudev, I bow to you again and again! You are the highest of all deities. You are the morning sun of intellect. O King of all Gurus! You are the only source of joy. You are the ultimate resting place of all. You alone grant Self-realization. You are the ocean from which the waves of creation arise, making diverse forms composed of the five elements. Your Siddhahood is supremely independent!

191.   It is God who rises in the form of the sun. He dwells in the hearts of all beings and in the thousand-rayed tendencies of the mind. He illumines the three states and the three worlds. He causes lost souls to return to Him. The power of the Siddhas' grace cures one's forgetfulness. Then the awareness of the all-pervasive Consciousness arises automatically.

192.   The Lord of Consciousness compels all 8,400,000 species of creatures to dance on the stage of the outer world. Each one dances its own strange dance as if in a movie. He has adorned each of them, from Brahmā to an insect, with a body according to its individual needs. Each creature becomes stiff with ego, forgets its own Self, and suffers. Through the

wisdom of the Siddhas, a person regains his knowledge of the Self and becomes the embodiment of supreme bliss. After he becomes established in perfection, no matter what he may perceive through his eyes or his intellect, he no longer distinguishes between himself and what he sees. His vision reveals to him his own true nature. A person who looks in a mirror sees his own face, which existed even before he looked in the mirror. Similarly, wherever a Siddha looks, he sees his own Self, which is without beginning.

193.   When that which is seen disappears, nothing remains except the seer. The act of seeing also vanishes. For example, a person dreams that he is embracing his friend, but when he awakens there is neither friend nor embrace, and he naturally becomes still. To experience perfection is the glorious result of a Siddha's grace. Then, no matter what a person may see or experience, he perceives the same thing in all. He acquires the vision which penetrates beyond the distinction of seer and the seen. Just as the sky is full of itself and therefore remains motionless, similarly, once a person fully enters the Self, he never moves from that state. This is the sign of Siddhahood.

194.   At the end of each world cycle, only water remains. Because it fills all space, there is no current or movement within it. In the same way, when the Self is full of itself, there is only stillness. How can fire devour itself? How can water bathe itself? Likewise, when a Siddha yogi becomes one with the Self of all, his coming and going ceases. The culmination of the journey to perfection is the cessation of all actions.

195.   In the ocean, there is only water. The waves which arise from one place and fall somewhere else are water. That

which creates this movement is also water. No matter how high waves may leap, they cannot go beyond the ocean shores. However high the tide may be, its essence, water, remains unaffected. The basic unity of the ocean is never destroyed. Similarly, when one attains Siddhahood, the bondage of duality ceases to exist.

196.   However firmly embedded the awareness of one's individuality may be, it ultimately merges into Consciousness. For this reason, one is always a pilgrim journeying toward Consciousness. Even if the needs of the body force a person to perform actions, he still ultimately attains the Lord of Consciousness. At that point, the ideas of doer and action vanish. Seeing only his own Self as Consciousness everywhere, a person becomes God. This is the Siddha's attainment of the knowledge of perfection.

197.   How can a mirror see itself? Why would one cover gold with gold plate? When a flame is already burning, a second flame cannot illumine it. In the same way, whatever a Siddha may do can never be considered action. To his vision, everything is That, neither good nor bad. This is the nature of perfect Siddhahood.

198.   Since a Siddha sees all actions and their results as God, how can he be said to perform actions? This state is known as supreme devotion to God and as the knowledge of the enlightened beings. A Siddha may appear to perform actions, but in fact he does not. Whatever he does is his worship of God. Whatever he says is a hymn of praise to Him. Whatever he sees, he sees as God. Wherever he walks, it is his pilgrimage to the supreme, divine unity. O friend, this is how a Siddha lives.

199. Because a Siddha's vision embodies the Absolute, whatever he does is worship of the Lord of Consciousness. Whatever thought of the outer world he may hold in his mind is repetition of God's name. If a Siddha remains still, his stillness is the state of *samādhi*. O friend, understand that just as a gold bracelet never becomes different from gold, a Siddha, through knowledge, devotion, and yoga, constantly remains united with God. This is the vision of the Siddhas.

200. O friend, as waves are in water, fragrance in camphor, and brilliance in jewels, so a Siddha dwells in supreme unity. As warp and woof are inseparable from cloth, as clay is inseparable from pots, so a Siddha is entirely one with God. A Siddha yogi who has attained complete knowledge of That remains inseparably immersed in Consciousness; he is the Self of the universe. Perceiving only Consciousness, he knows the seer as it is. Through his awareness of the Self in all objects, he knows the true nature of the seen. You may call this state madness. O friend, correct your vision. Cure your own madness. Through the meditation and knowledge of the Siddhas, you will realize, "I was the one who was deluded."

201. The following story makes an important point: Once there lived a crow king and an owl king. Both had many companions. They lived with their friends in the same forest on their respective trees. One day they met, and the crow asked, "Why do you work at night?" The owl protested, "O brother, it is you who works at night." This began a long, heated argument. As they argued, the day wore on and became night. The owl said, "O king of the crows, now it is day." The crow replied, "No, brother, it is night." Then they began to fight in earnest.

At that point, a swan arrived and said, "Don't fight. You

are both right. What is day for a crow is night for an owl. What is day for an owl is night for a crow."

In the same way, an ignorant person's day of sense pleasures and possessions is night for a Siddha and is to be renounced. What is day for a Siddha — his awareness of the Self of all, the knowledge of "I am That," and the understanding of the all-pervasive light of bliss — is night for an ignorant person. Turn your night into day. Muktānanda says, "Then Siddha Yoga is filled with ecstasy and joy."

202.   The wise person who has attained Siddhahood sees that he himself, the seer, is the entire universe. Having attained this wisdom and the experience of the Self in this very body, he begins to dance with joy. He comes to the conclusion that what he had perceived as a snake is nothing but a rope. When his Kundalinī is awakened and he totally merges with Shiva, his inner experience illumines his outer world as well. Then he has the outlook of a Siddha.

203.   When gold ornaments are melted, it becomes obvious that even in name they were never different from gold. When a seeker understands that waves consist of nothing but water, he never again considers their forms to be either lasting in themselves or separate from the ocean. Similarly, through the grace of a Siddha, the wisdom of the Siddhas arises from within, and one feels, "Ah, I am all this!"

204.   When a person awakens, he is no longer aware of the various ramblings of his dreams. He is conscious only of his waking state. Similarly, a Siddha forgets the dream of bondage and understands that he, the knower, is everything visible and invisible — all objects, the process of knowing, all that there is. He experiences: "I am the knower. I am

unborn, deathless, indestructible, and inexhaustible. I am primordial, limitless bliss." This is the true understanding of Siddha Yoga.

205. A Siddha has this continual awareness: "That conscious Being is ancient. He is both unmanifest and manifest. I am controlled by the Supreme Power, and I am the controller as well. That Supreme Power is beginningless, indestructible, and fearless. It is both the support and that which is supported. I am self-born and exist in all forms as the inner Self. I am also beyond everything. I am new as well as old. I am the void as well as the whole. I am both large and small. I am every existing thing." This is the statement of the Siddhas.

206. "I am a Siddha and exist everywhere equally. I am filled with Consciousness." Through God's grace and his one-pointed devotion, a Siddha truly knows this. He is also aware that he is the knowledge of the experience of the Self. Just as an ignorant person naturally identifies himself with the body, a Siddha fully experiences himself as the embodiment of bliss. A Siddha lives in total freedom.

207. A person who has a nightmare becomes terrified. He awakens with a start and asks those around him, "Where did the three-horned tiger go?" He creates his own dream images and then fears them, but both the dream and the fear vanish when he awakens. Likewise, a Siddha yogi becomes serene, carefree, and pure when he perceives the universe within himself. Then he spontaneously retains the experience of perfection.

208. Not only does the rising sun reveal the world, it also reveals itself. This illustrates how the revealer and what is revealed are one and the same. Similarly, when both knowl-

edge and ignorance vanish, only the Knower remains. When a person fully understands this, he himself becomes the Knower. Siddha Yoga has unlimited power to grant one the vision of one's own Self.

209.   Only one who has the supreme knowledge of unity and equality can know the state of an enlightened being. A Siddha understands that he himself is the force behind that power of knowledge. He also understands that he is the principle of the Self, beyond both unity and duality, beyond the beyond. There is no doubt about this. When a person awakens from sleep, for a moment he is aware only of himself. The state of a being who experiences direct knowledge is permanently like this. He becomes calm and attains the Siddhas' awareness of equality.

210.   Someone once asked Saint Tukārām, "What is the state of a saint, a great soul, an enlightened being, a Siddha? What is his experience?" Tukārām Mahārāj replied, "If you want to know how a fish sleeps in water, you will have to become a fish." Just as a fish lives immersed in water so, when a person becomes established in the state of a Siddha, his whole being is immersed in his own true nature. One cannot understand his state of being. Only a Siddha can know it.

211.   When Maharishi Nārada was asked this question about the state of a saint, he replied, "A devotee is wholly immersed in Consciousness and has lost himself in it." When they are heated, gold ornaments melt but remain gold. When salt dissolves in water, it seems to disappear, but the salty taste remains. Similarly, even though a Siddha has the awareness, "I am the Supreme Absolute," and merges into the nectar of ecstasy, he still experiences his own bliss and becomes serene. This is the state of the Siddhas.

212. As long as Lord Krishna was with Arjuna, Arjuna was victorious in many battles. He was considered an illustrious man. He was so worthy that the Lord revealed to him the secret knowledge behind the mystery of the Vedas and showed him His universal form.

Many years later, Krishna left this earth. For so long, because of Krishna's physical presence, Arjuna had felt secure in Krishna's grace. But now he thought the Lord was dead and he became filled with sorrow. At this time, Arjuna was in charge of escorting some of the Lord's people to another town. Suddenly some tribal boys attacked them and began to rob the women. To his horror, Arjuna discovered that he was powerless to stop them. That same Arjuna with his powerful bow and arrows was incapable of preventing the robbery.

O my friend, Arjuna's victories had never been due to his bravery but to Krishna's grace. Because of his wrong understanding of the Lord's true nature, Arjuna lost all his strength and became weak. Even a single thought of Krishna would have been enough to give him strength, but now ordinary tribal boys defeated him. He did not remember Krishna, so he no longer had Krishna's grace.

Remember that as long as Shrī Guru's grace and compassion are with Muktānanda, he is fine. Otherwise, he is worth only a penny. Protect your right understanding. Discard the ego which you have hidden behind your knowledge. You may think that it is well concealed, but your ego is betraying you.

The Siddhas' behavior toward others is pure and totally free of deception. Always contemplate their nonattachment, their awareness of equality, and their true love for all. Then the Siddhas' grace will awaken in you.

213. The Supreme Being is inherent in all that one does. He sees all one's actions and immediately determines their fruits. If one plants strawberries, one will not harvest apples. A cat

eats with its eyes closed and thinks that no one can see it. O cat, you may have closed your eyes, but the eyes of the Witness remain open. One's actions are the Absolute itself. They create one's heaven and hell. Be vigilant. Be pure within and without. Know that only then will you come closer to discovering the secret of the Siddhas. Remember this.

214.   As I mentioned before, the divine sage Nārada said, "A devotee is wholly immersed in Consciousness." When a yogi enters the supreme light of the Absolute, he relinquishes all notions of himself and others. His former idea of "I" and "that" is annihilated. He merges into his own true nature and becomes perfect. Such a great being does not become an inflated ego-balloon. He does not flaunt himself, saying, "I saw myself above the seventh heaven." He does not stretch out his begging bowl and say, "Call me God." A being who is fearful and depends on bodyguards to protect him cannot be God, nor can one who has to be locked up in a mental hospital to cool down his deranged mind. Shaivism says, *Siddhaha svatantrabhāvaha* — "A Siddha lives in total freedom."[23]

215.   For a great being, there is no attachment, no enmity, no delusion, and no fear. He merges all his different "therapies" into the space of Consciousness. He does not perceive any stench in others. He becomes one with the awareness of equality. He does not drink the foul poison of criticizing others, nor does he quietly burn inwardly in the fire of enmity and jealousy when he sees or hears of others' greatness. It is astonishing: If one crow gets a morsel of food, all the other crows pursue him. For the same reason, a vulture chases another vulture, or a mongrel trails another mongrel. In the jungle, one animal is always waiting to prey upon another. If

---

23. *Shiva Sūtras*, III-13.

a being is in the same state as these animals, he is neither God, nor a Siddha, a *sādhu*,[24] a swāmi, or a noble person. O my friends, think about this. What is Siddhahood?

216.   When camphor begins to burn, one can see a flame. When both the camphor and the flame vanish, only space remains. When one subtracts one from one, nothing is left. In the same way, when one discards one's ideas about what exists and what does not exist, of what is present and what is not present, all that remains is Truth and infinite bliss. This state is not a piano of ego on which one plays *do, re, mi, fa, sol, la, ti, do.* In this state, even such words as the Absolute, the Self, and God obstruct one's bliss; there is not even any room to say, "Nothing exists here." This is the state the Siddhas have attained.

217.   The state of a Siddha is beyond both knowing and not knowing. In that state, bliss is embraced with bliss. Joy is experienced through joy. Success is gained through success. Light dwells within light. Shaivism says that the stages of yoga are filled with amazing phenomena.[25] In that state, astonishment drowns in astonishment. All dos and don'ts are silenced. Rest attains total rest. Experience delights in experience. The state of a Siddha is the attainment of total perfection. Siddhas are like this. O friend, read this very carefully.

218.   One who constantly practices the disciplines of Siddha Yoga and performs noble actions attains the pure fruit of the nature of the Self. It can be understood in this way. Imagine

---

24. Holy man.
25. *Shiva Sūtras*, I-12.

that Siddha Yoga is a temple and that liberation, the final attainment of Siddha Yoga, is the crown of the dome of that temple. Know that when the yogi reaches that crown, he becomes as all-pervading as the sky above the dome.

It can also be understood in another way. Siddha Yoga is a broad stream through the forest of the world. This stream leads to the realm of oneness, where the individual soul and the Absolute merge. Through knowledge, devotion, and yoga, a person is swiftly carried along by the current and merges into the ocean of bliss, the name of God. Then a Siddha yogi becomes an exalted being. This is why I have written at length about him.

8

The Guru is the Means

219. Now, after discussing the Supreme Principle in detail, we will turn to *sādhanā*, or the means of attaining that Principle. The Supreme Principle is not something one attains by doing *sādhanā* in the right place at the right time. Consciousness is complete within itself and exists in all eternally. Shaivism teaches that this entire world is the play of Consciousness. For this reason, one does not have to undergo any kind of difficulty to attain God. Through Siddha Yoga, one automatically attains the principle of the Self. Siddha Yoga is effortless and simple.

220. It is universally true that in all fields, if there is a student, then there must also be a teacher. In this world, there is a teacher for every subject. This is nothing new. If there is a music student, there is also a music teacher. If there is a patient, there is also an acupuncturist, a healer, or a psychic who perceives the unseen. Similarly, if there is a spiritual seeker, there must also be a guide to point out the right path. In Siddha Yoga, the Siddha Guru guides the seeker unerringly.

On the Siddha Path, one needs a Guru who has been chosen by another Siddha of the true lineage of Siddhas. He must have complete knowledge and be proficient at transmitting energy and removing all obstacles. He should always be pure, simple, and straightforward, capable of bestowing wisdom and making love flow. He must know that true Principle just as it is. He must have become one with That. He should be content with whatever comes to him and free of addictions. He must also be a master of diplomacy. One needs a Guru who can point out the path to attain the Self, but in addition one has to put forth self-effort.

221.   Treasures lie in the womb of the earth, fire is latent in wood, and milk is in the udder of a cow. However, one has to take certain actions to acquire them. In the same way, even though the Supreme Principle is within us, a person who wishes to attain it must use the right means. This is necessary because we have been going in the wrong direction for such a long time. Even a person of discrimination and exalted vision must make some effort in order for that Principle to manifest for him completely.

222.   One's hands can remove moss from water, but they cannot create water. Forgetfulness of one's true nature is the moss of ignorance which muddies the experience of the Self. The Guru is the means of removing it. Just as the wind disperses the clouds but does not create another blazing sun, so the grace of a Siddha simply removes the veil of ignorance so that one realizes that one is already perfect. Consciousness, or the awareness "I am perfect," always remains pure and radiant. For this reason, all scriptures and sādhanās are simply means of washing away the filth of ignorance. They have no ability of their own to reveal the wisdom of the Self because that Principle is self-existent, perfect, and always manifest.

   How the Siddhas attain that state of Truth is the mystery of yoga. When the sun rises in the east, all other directions are illumined with brilliant light. In the same way, when the

Siddhas follow this exalted path, the Supreme Principle manifests of its own accord. I repeat this again and again in great detail for the benefit of the seeker who is engaged in *sādhanā*. It will enable him to know the Truth and thus become happy and carefree. He will realize how easy it is to reach that state without getting lost or going in the wrong direction. The Siddha Path is so simple that he will instantly reach his true state.

223. Constant and independent contentment is the sign of a being who has attained That. When a seeker becomes worthy of attaining the Absolute, his mind becomes unshakable and contented. The path of the Siddhas leads to the wisdom of the Supreme Principle. During the rainy season there are floods, but in autumn the river becomes quiet and its turbulence calms down. At the end of a song, the accompanying drum beat dies out. In the same way, one's striving and tension vanish the moment one attains Self-realization. The serenity and joy of this state are the glory of Self-realization. At this point, one is flooded with the awareness of inner contentment. A fountain of joy wells up in one's heart when one's awareness becomes stable. Then one has attained Siddhahood. One is awarded the highest certificate from the Siddha University. O friend, make sure that you get the right certificate.

224. When the sun rises, all the stars fade away in its brilliance. Similarly, when the sun of knowledge rises in the heart and a person experiences the essence of the Self, the universe of diversity with its countless beings and objects is dissolved for him. Duality perishes. The radiant sun of the Self blazes in his eyes. Its flame radiates through every pore of his body. As it flashes, his entire body is filled with the nectar of love. Drops of nectar from the stream of love flow from his eyes.

His words shower love. His speech is never an arrow which pierces others' hearts with bitter, cruel, or filthy words. The wisdom of the Siddhas is sweet.

225.   When one is initiated into *sannyāsa*, one dons clothing of radiant orange. Similarly, as love shimmers within a swāmi, his speech, language, and understanding become clothed with sweetness. He looks upon everyone with love. Harsh words are a sign of inner dryness. Self-praise is evidence of nonattainment. Cruelty is proof of hatred. The idea of differences indicates the cancer of ignorance. Living in the midst of people, a swāmi loves all but remains independent of everyone. He gives up all expectations. True *sannyāsa* spontaneously makes a swāmi a natural renunciant. In Muktānanda's words, it is not enough merely to play the role of a *sannyāsin*. A real *sannyāsin* belongs to the Nandapadma Order.

226.   O friend! A person may claim to be a great being, a Siddha, or a leader. He may be a performer of miracles. He may claim to hold the degree of God. But if he does not behave properly, he will lead people astray. The behavior of a great being is the greatest example for others, and they follow it. Become true, sublime, perfect, and pure. Never lead people in the wrong direction. Muktānanda welcomes you all from his own Self. For me, true Guruhood is God.

227.   Every person has some addiction. He loves that addiction and makes it his intimate friend. In India, there is a particular group of proverbs about addictions, which are true as well as witty. One of them is: "The sun loves salutations." In Hatha Yoga, the salutation to the sun is a very important exercise. When I was in Miami Beach, I saw that every man, woman, and child had so much respect for the sun that they

lay outside for hours on end. Perhaps this was their way of showing love and devotion to the sun!

There is another saying: "Lord Vishnu likes ornaments." In India, people adorn the temples of Vishnu with great splendor. In America, there are also countless varieties of ornamentation: Out of self-respect, people beautify themselves with plastic surgery, numerous types of makeup, and fashionable clothes. I have gained a great deal of understanding from all of this. The whole world is imitating Vishnu's love of ornaments. Go ahead and adorn yourself. But remember, do not throw the wisdom of Vishnu into the garbage can. His Self is within you. I tell everyone, "It is not enough just to imitate Vishnu outwardly. Adorn the inner Vishnu as well. The cosmetic shop is within." Siddha Yoga tells everyone to go to that shop.

A third saying is: "Shiva loves a ritual bath." The Indians worship Shiva in the form of a *lingam* by giving it a ritual bath. As they recite mantras, they pour over it yogurt, milk, honey, coconut water, and other delicious liquids. If the worshipper does this with the feeling that God is everywhere, He will receive these offerings. God is pleased if the worshipper is contented. We imitate this Shiva worship. We give ourselves ritual "baths" with Coca-Cola, lemonade, orange juice, brandy, or vodka. Some are intoxicating and others are not. Remember that Shiva is also within the inner heart. Give Him a ritual bath there as well. Bathe Him with ever-increasing love, which is sweet and nectarean. The intoxication of inner love will arise, and you yourself will become Shiva.

228. O friend, everyone in the world has one addiction or another. I also have an addiction which I cherish, and that is Shrī Gurudev. I am very fond of saying, *Sadgurunāth Mahārāj ki Jai!* I dearly love to gaze at his face. I am also addicted to repeating *Guru Om, Guru Om.*

Tukārām Mahārāj was addicted to chanting. Nāmadev was addicted to singing the divine name. Mīrābāi was addicted to putting on anklets and dancing and chanting with the intoxication of love. Sūradās was addicted to devotion. Ekanāth Mahārāj was addicted to devotion to the Guru. Jnāneshwar Mahārāj was addicted to knowledge of God and the Guru. Even after attaining perfection, these saints still had their addictions. In the same way, I am addicted to my Guru. Wherever I go to eat, bathe, sleep, or give darshan, I like to have a beautiful picture of him before me.

But the guru market is down, not only in America but throughout the world. The moment a person hears the word "guru," he becomes upset. If anyone mentions the word "guru" to his family or displays a guru's photographs, he is considered crazy. Young boys and girls may go anywhere — to a theater, movie, or nightclub to drink beer or brandy. They may go with their friends wherever they want, and their families will give them money and credit cards for their expenses. But they place one condition on this: They must not go to a guru or chant God's name. If the boys and girls do not listen, their families take away their credit cards. They get people to convince them not to go to a guru.

Why is the guru market so low these days? It is because gurus do not behave properly. Of course, some gurus are true. In all fields, there are both the genuine and the false, so it is not at all remarkable that there are also false gurus. Nevertheless, when people are deceived and suffer loss, it is only because of their wrong understanding. One finds a guru who is like oneself. One accepts a guru according to one's own nature. So says Muktānanda.

229.   There are different religions, such as Sufism, Christianity, Hinduism, and Judaism. There are rabbis, Moslem priests, ayatullahs, and popes. There are also different lineages which originated from Gurus who were true and intelligent.

The Guru's position is lofty, noble, and worthy of respect. Lord Krishna's Guru was Sāndīpani. Shrī Rām's Guru was Vasishtha. Kabir's Guru was Rāmānanda. There were Shankarāchārya, Guru Nānakdev, and Jesus; their power is still actively functioning in the world. There were swamis of the Nandapadma Order whose teachings were sublime. They were boats in which people crossed over the ocean of worldliness. The passage on those boats was guaranteed. Those who sailed on them had no fear because those great Gurus always took a person to the final goal. Guruhood is not an evil thing, but if a person makes himself a guru without having attained Guruhood, then his boat sinks, and the guru market goes down.

230. I do not put pressure on anyone. Siddha Yoga is not a guru cult. But in every field, one needs a guide. On the spiritual path, too, a Guru is necessary. At certain times in one's life, healers, psychologists, psychics, and professors may all be necessary. In the same way, in spiritual life, one needs a guide who is wise and compassionate, who observes good conduct, who has studied the scriptures and spiritual philosophies, and who has understood the Truth. He should have been the disciple of a spiritual leader who incorporated scriptural injunctions into his own life.

Whatever anyone may say or think about me, I take great interest in my Guru. My love for him has become an addiction. That Siddha gave me one word[26] which completely transformed me, but I had to spend such a long time with him to receive it. That word which I received after so many years spread through my body from head to toe like wildfire carried by the wind. It produced in me both inner heat and the coolness of joy.

---

26. The mantra.

Before meeting my Guru, I had practiced many different kinds of yoga, but it was I who had practiced them. However, that word activated a spontaneous yoga within me. I was filled with amazement. What postures, *mudrās*, and breathing processes! Everything happened on its own. After attaining divine realization, I understood my compassionate Guru.

231. After the awakening of the Shakti, this process of yogic movements began to take place within my entire body. What power that word had! I almost hesitate to write all of this. It revealed whatever was within me — in my heart and in my head. I saw my own double many times. In the *sahasrāra* at the crown of the head, I perceived the brilliance of a thousand suns. I also saw the Blue Being. Sometimes I would lose myself within; then I would regain consciousness. It was like a play, similar to that of the waking and dream states. Even now, I do not know where I lose my small self and from where it returns. It is so amusing — I lose myself, then find myself. I have seen the center of true joy; there I lose myself and from there I return. I am ecstatic! I have found the best place of all, right within myself.

232. I have rediscovered that which I never lost. Still, my addiction has not left me. Jai Gurudev! Such a great addiction to the Guru! *Guru Om!* The repetition of this great mantra occurs even in my dreams. I do not know who repeats it there. My Guru's picture seems to come alive for me. When I look at his eyes, I see radiance. When I gaze at his body, it seems to be moving. When I look at his face, a smile seems to play on his lips. People may think this is madness. So be it. How beautiful! How exquisite! How ecstatic! Sometimes in the privacy of my room, I dance while singing *Guru Om, Guru Om*. Sometimes I feel that my beloved's head is swaying in the photograph. Such madness of love

arises within me! The pulsation of his ecstasy pervades my entire body like the movement of the wind. I have become what I wanted to become. Still, my addiction has never left me. The blessings of the Guru are wondrous and extraordinary.

233. How did I become so hopelessly addicted? After pondering this question for a long time, I finally realized that he himself had entered me through my ear in the form of that word. The power of the Self had entered me. The *kriyās* were his, the yoga was his, and meditation took place because of him. It was he, the embodiment of Consciousness, who emerged from the Blue Pearl. The final message which I received was from him. I have come to understand that he is the bliss of infinity, the bliss of love, the bliss of perfection, the bliss of the Supreme, and the bliss of the Self. What an extraordinary discovery!

234. Now I completely understand my addiction. It is his radiance in the light of my eyes. It is his utterance in the speech of my tongue. Through my breathing, it is he who comes in and goes out. It is he who eats, drinks, hears, and makes me hear. The power of his word permeates each of my blood cells. The fluids of my entire body are his. That is why I am joyful. I now understand that what I considered to be myself was totally unreal. I had made an error in calculation and was trapped in it. The truth is that Gurudev himself had entered me through that word.

235. Ah, what power that word had! Gurudev entered me and replaced all my bodily fluids with his. How powerful he is! He evicted me and took up residence himself. He annihilated my ego. Now I understand that this was why I became addicted to him. Once Sheik Nāsrudīn wore someone else's coat and claimed that it belonged to him. This is not like

that. My Guru entered me, and who knows where he disposed of me? By making my individuality his, he became me. This is the Guru's compassion.

236.   My attainment is Gurudev. My *sādhanā* is Gurudev. My realization is Gurudev. My mantra is Gurudev. What is the formless or the attributeless? What is realization of the form? It is all delusion created by words. When two sticks are rubbed together, an exquisite flame arises. By the churning of milk, butter is produced. Similarly, joy arises from the love of *Guru Om* and from the churning of the love between the Guru and the disciple. Only the Guru can know that delight and taste the elixir which arises in every pore of the body. This love cannot be attained through practicing yoga, through indulging in sense pleasures, or through prattling about knowledge.

Only when a river merges into the ocean can it fully know the splendor of the ocean. Only when I lost myself in the ecstasy of Nityānanda did I realize who he was. He is the nectar of love which arises when everything, sentient and insentient, becomes one. He is the beauty of the world. He pervades all forms, conscious and inert. He is the luminous sun, the moon, and the stars in the heavens. He frolics and sways with love in the blowing of the wind. His consciousness glimmers in men and women. There is only Nityānanda, nothing but Nityānanda. He is the bliss of the Absolute, the bliss of the Self, the bliss of freedom, and the bliss of love. There is only love, love, nothing but love.

Book II

Philosophy of the Siddhas

9

The Origin of Kashmir Shaivism

237. Now I shall write briefly about the essence of Kashmir Shaivism. Supreme Shiva Himself gave birth to the Shaiva philosophy, and Vasuguptāchārya, a great Siddha being and the head of a distinguished lineage, elaborated it. Shaivism teaches that Shiva and Shakti are the cause of the universe. They are not two but one. Shaivism tells us that Shiva is static, attributeless, and formless and that Shakti is His dynamic aspect. Shiva is the seeker's ultimate goal.

238. This Shiva, who is also called Srīkantha, is the Primordial Being of Shaivism. From Shiva came Vasugupta, Somānanda, Utpalāchārya, Lakshmanagupta, Rāmakantha, Abhinavagupta, Kshemarāja, Yogarāja, Kallata, Pradyumna Bhatta, Prajnārjuna, Mahādeva Bhatta, Shrīkantha Bhatta, Bhāskara, and other Siddhas. This lineage originating from Shiva has existed since time immemorial.

There were also many yogis who came from Shiva, one of whom was Durvāsa. He created three sons, Tryambaka, Amardaka, and Shrīnātha, through the power of his mind. The history of all these beings is vast, profound, and highly secret. It would take great effort to write such a lengthy history. Seekers do not need to know it. We should neither waste our time nor lose faith and trust by discussing the origin of rivers and great beings. These investigations only add to our doubts.

239. Why should we know the origin of rivers? Our duty is to bathe in them, to wash away our impurities, and to cool the heat of our bodies. In the same way, it is our duty to understand the sages, to contemplate their teachings, and to practice the *sādhanā* which they have shown us. It is our duty to attain our own divinity, to become happy in the bliss of reunion with the Self, and to lead our lives with great freedom and joy. Above all, our task is to complete our journey to the Self. Harboring unnecessary doubts makes a person fall from the path.

240. The principal scripture of Shaivism is the *Shiva Sūtras*. These teachings were revealed by Shiva and kept highly secret until the great Siddha Vasugupta disseminated them throughout the world. Many Siddhas in Vasugupta's lineage wrote works based on the *Shiva Sūtras*.

241. The *Shiva Sūtras* describe three *upāyas*, or means of *sādhanā* — *shāmbhava upāya*, *shākta upāya*, and *āṇava upāya*. These three *upāyas* were established in the *Shiva Sūtras* to suit the temperaments, qualities, and natures of different people and enable them to attain the same Self.

242. The sages described the characteristics of a *sūtra* as follows: *Alpāksharamasandigdham*[27] This means that a *sūtra* should contain very few words but should leave no room for doubt.

---

27. *Padma Purāna.*

A *sūtra* should capture the essence of the principle it discusses. It should provide satisfactory solutions to problems according to the time and place. *Sūtras* should neither be contradictory nor give misinformation. Some *sūtras* are so pithy that they are unclear even to great scholars. At such times, one needs the help of an experienced Guru.

243. The *Shiva Sūtras* consist of seventy-seven *sūtras* written in simple language and divided into three sections. The first section contains the *sūtras* belonging to the *shāmbhava upāya*, the second to the *shākta upāya*, and the third to the *ānava upāya*. Originally, Gurus taught these *sūtras* to their disciples orally and in secret. Later, the great being Vasugupta wrote them down and disseminated them throughout the world. Now they are easily accessible. They are Vasugupta's great gift to us. We offer our salutations at his feet.

244. Seekers should assimilate completely the essence of the *Shiva Sūtras*. They should make an effort to acquire the ability to digest them entirely. The subject should not give them dysentery.

10

Shāmbhava Upāya

245. In mundane matters, one's feelings and thoughts are important. In spiritual matters, however, one must transcend thoughts and feelings in order to discover and recognize the Supreme Principle which is their source. If one contemplates the purpose of life, the question inevitably arises, "What is its origin?"

246. Some people think that life is merely entertainment, that it is meant for indulging in sense pleasures and obtaining wealth, fame, power, and limitless enjoyments. Driven by the restlessness of the monkey-mind, they eat, drink, dance, jump around, and ultimately destroy their priceless life. Then, crying out and weeping, they continually repent. They blame time, destiny, their parents, relatives, and national policies. Finally, they become death's victims. This is a complete map of the journey through the world.

247. When a person is seeking knowledge of the origin of life and begins to understand its reality, he occasionally loses interest in mundane matters. Sometimes he thinks that

worldly knowledge may be an impediment to the realization of Truth. This kind of thinking occurs because of his partial or limited knowledge of the Truth.

If one does not have complete knowledge of the Truth and performs actions without proper understanding, attachment and aversion can arise. This happens because of ignorance of one's own Self and of the true nature of the world, as well as because of the wild, destructive dance of one's inner fantasies. The *Shiva Sūtras* describe this condition in the aphorism *Jnānam bandhaha*[28] — "[Limited] knowledge is bondage."

248. Paramashiva or Parāsamvit, who contains various powers and whose nature is Consciousness, is the Supreme Principle. It is described in the first of the *Shiva Sūtras: Chaitanyam ātmā* — "The Self is Consciousness." In truth, there is nothing other than that conscious light, which is the Ultimate Reality. This world is the play of that Principle, the Universal Consciousness.

249. Paramashiva Himself, by contracting according to His own will, has brought about the effects of the three impurities — *ānava mala*, *māyīya mala*, and *kārma mala*.[29] This is His game, drama, entertainment, journey, picnic, and sport. It is neither real nor unreal.

250. Enveloped in the three impurities, the individual soul falls under the influence of the letters, or sound-syllables, which are the basis of words. From these letters comes language, from language come ideas, and from ideas comes the understanding "I am imperfect." This notion brings about the

---

28. *Shiva Sūtras*, I-2.
29. See Glossary.

limitation of one's power. Therefore, this kind of understanding is bondage. Shaivism describes this state by saying,
Jnānam bandhaha and *Jnānādhishthānam mātrikā*[30] —"Limited knowledge arises from the *mātrikā shakti.*"[31]

251. Many factors contribute to the functioning of a human
being, including the body, the senses, the mind, and the
various gross and subtle principles. The understanding derived from all these instruments and principles takes a form
and, so that others can understand it, manifests outwardly as
groups of letters in the form of language. These letters arise
from a source known as the *mātrikā chakra.*[32]

252. A seeker who pursues the Truth knows that everything,
from the gross body to the *mātrikā chakra*, is nothing but a
group of powers, or *shaktis*. His main duty is to recognize the
Supreme Principle, which is the source of this group of
powers. It is not possible to recognize the Supreme Principle
through the senses. The Supreme Light can be recognized
only through the purified willpower. When one contemplates the Supreme Principle, one perceives that all the
activities of the entire world occur because of the pulsation
and play of Parāshakti. By inwardly contemplating his
identity with the Supreme Principle, a Siddha neither rejects
nor hates the activities of the outer world. Instead, he
participates in them fully.

---

30. *Shiva Sūtras*, I-4.

31. *Mātrikā shakti* is the power of letters, the subtle vibration of Shakti which arises
as the letters of the alphabet. It is the source of the entire inner experience of an
individual. All the letters of the Sanskrit alphabet from *a* to *ksha* are referred to as
mātrikās. However, the basic principle of *mātrikā* applies equally to all languages.

32. The supreme power of Consciousness in its primal sound form from which all
mātrikās arise.

253.   One should always remember that a human being has four
       bodies. In the physical body, one experiences the waking
       state and performs mundane activities. Some of these ac-
       tivities are re-experienced in the subtle body in the dream
       state, but since this state lacks any independent content, the
       experiences in this state cannot be called real.
           The goals and conflicts of the waking state are not per-
       ceived at all in the state of deep sleep because in that state
       there are neither feelings nor mental activity. This state lies
       beyond the dream state and corresponds to the third, or
       causal, body.

254.   The state which pertains to the fourth body is called *turīya*.
       It is invaluable. In this state, one recognizes one's Self, one's
       own true nature; this can be recognized only through inner
       experience, not through the senses. Trying to describe this
       state is like a mute person trying to describe the sweets he is
       eating. Jnāneshwar Mahārāj said, "You can attain that state
       only by stealing it from all the senses."

255.   The Self, one's own true nature, is essentially Conscious-
       ness, or God; for that reason, *icchā, jnāna,* and *kriyā shaktis*
       exist in it. Through *icchā shakti* — the power of will — the
       bliss of the *turīya* state can be recognized. It cannot be
       perceived through any other kind of understanding. The
       bliss of *turīya* exists within us at all times; it is that which
       makes us take interest in different things. To know the *turīya*
       state is to realize the Truth. It is a sublime and blissful state.

256.   A realized yogi assimilates this intense bliss by remaining
       in the *turīya* state all the time. He himself becomes that bliss.
       He does not have to subdue his senses; where can the poor
       senses go to escape that all-pervasive ocean of bliss? By

freeing himself from attachment and aversion and by detaching himself from praise and blame, that yogi experiences his own Self. Such a yogi is called Vīresha, the lord of the senses. He experiences wonder at the adventure of the universe. His *icchā shakti* has transcended all limitations.

257. Through the understanding that he has gained from being centered in the Self, his former idea of duality, of "I" and "this," merges into the bliss of the Self. Through his *icchā shakti*, spontaneous knowledge of equality arises within. Such a yogi experiences the all-pervasive unity in himself and in everything that he perceives. He attains the power to create an inner world through his will. Various miraculous and supernatural powers come to him. By constantly pursuing the Supreme Principle, he experiences the divine "I"-consciousness which empowers the mantra. That power removes all bondage and establishes one in the *turīya* state. It is also called Shakti or *mudrā vīrya*, that which dissolves bondage.

258. When, through the power of *icchā shakti*, one has the experience "I am not different from the Supreme Principle," this is called *shāmbhava upāya*.

> *Akinchit chintakasyaiva gurunā pratibodhataha,*
> *Yam samāveshamāpnoti shāmbhavo' sāvudāhritaha.* [33]

> Absorption in Shiva-consciousness comes to one whose mind has become free of thought as a result of an awakening by the Guru or through an intense spontaneous awakening.

In the *shāmbhava upāya*, *sādhanā* and the goal of *sādhanā* are one; therefore, this is also called the *abheda upāya*, or the

---

33. Kshemarāja, *Shiva Sūtra Vimarshinī.*

nondual means. Because in this *upāya* the Supreme can be attained through *icchā shakti*, it is sometimes referred to as the *icchā upāya*, or the means of pure will. Primarily, the *sūtras* of the *shāmbhava upāya* discuss such subjects as the nature of bondage, the four states (waking, dream, deep sleep, and *turīya*), the stages of yoga, the evolution of Consciousness, the bliss of *samādhi*, the acquisition of willpower, the upliftment of the world, and the attainment of the potency of the mantra.

259.   Through the wisdom of the Shakti, activated by Shrī Guru or through an intense spontaneous awakening, all thoughts cease. Such an experience is called the *shāmbhava samāvesha* or the *shāmbhava upāya*.

260.   By pursuing unity through the *shāmbhava upāya*, one sees the world as the play of the Self. Then wherever one looks, one sees only the play of Consciousness. One becomes like the *gopis*, who said, "Wherever I look, I see Shyām alone." In this state, wherever one looks, one sees nothing which is different from Shiva. One understands that it is Shiva who has assumed different forms within and without. He has become a man, a woman, and every other thing. Shiva is omniscient, omnipotent, and all-pervasive. He is the Supreme Principle. The experience that the world is the embodiment of Shiva is known as the *shāmbhava upāya*.

261.   The universe is a garden for us to roam in with love. It is not intended as a source of attachment, jealousy, hatred, or anxiety. These only destroy our equanimity. Give up all desires. If something comes, let it come; if something goes, let it go. It is all Shiva's play. This is not a mere universe; it is the image of Him. Knowing it as Shiva, love it. Meditate on

the awareness that all conscious beings as well as inert matter
are Shiva. Having the knowledge of Shiva, understand that
the world is the embodiment of Him. Take this kind of
sannyāsa. Shiva alone exists everywhere. Muktānanda,
know that this is the *shāmbhava upāya*.

11

Shākta Upāya

262.   There is only one Self in all human beings. However, the
upāyas, or means of reaching that Self, are different. This is
due to the three *gunas*,[34] or qualities — *sattva* (purity), *rajas*
(activity), and *tamas* (inertia) —as well as to the fact that
people have different temperaments, mental impurities,
karmic impressions from countless lifetimes, and various
kinds of understanding. In reality, all the *upāyas* are one.
Their techniques vary to suit the needs of different individuals, but they do not depart from their original purpose.

   In *shākta upāya*, one's awareness and feeling are paramount
because the *shāktā upāya* manifests through them. *Bhāve hi
vidyate devo* — "God exists in the form of feeling." The
Bhagavad Gītā says, *Madbhāva mānasā jāta* — "The world
exists in My feeling." The world is the embodiment of one's
feeling. All one's activities take place according to one's
understanding. One's feeling and opinions are mental tendencies. According to the tendencies of one's mind, a particular person is one's husband, wife, father, mother, son,

---

34. According to the Indian system, every creature, object, and state in the
material universe is composed of these three basic qualities of nature, in permuta-
tion and combination. For details, see the *Bhagavad Gītā* and other texts.

daughter, girlfriend, boyfriend, Guru, disciple, Bābā, or companion. But once one's feeling for that person wanes, the mind withdraws from the relationship. When one's love diminishes, one no longer recognizes that person. As far as one is concerned, the person whom one loved the most is dead while still alive.

There are countless mental tendencies. Although they seem to be positive or negative when they arise, once they merge into Consciousness they become one with it. The place where the mental tendencies arise and become dual is the same place where they merge and become nondual.

263. The main purpose of the *shākta upāya* is to obtain the experience of all-pervasive unity through the power of feeling. As one practices this *upāya*, one's thoughts gradually calm down, and one rejects the dualistic tendencies which exist in the ordinary state.

264. In this *upāya*, the mind is the instrument through which the Supreme Principle is pursued. The mind has the ability to erase an old way of looking at the world and to create a new relationship with a new world. Mantra is nondual contemplation directed within. Therefore, Shiva said, *Chittam mantraha*[35] — "The mind is mantra," and *Chetyate vimrishyate anena param tattvam iti chittam*[36] — "The mind is that which illumines and understands the highest Principle." It merges into the Supreme Principle and leads to recognition of That.

A seeker worships a deity through mantras. There is no difference between the seeker, the mantra, and the deity of the mantra. The main goal of the *shākta upāya* is to establish

---

35. *Shiva Sūtras*, II-1.

36. Kshemarāja, *Shiva Sūtra Vimarshinī*, commentary on II-1.

one in the awareness of the unity of these three. In the *shākta upāya*, one attempts to merge into the Supreme Light. *Prayatnaha sādhakaha*[37] — "Achievement comes through effort."

265. *Vidyā* is the highest knowledge of unity. Through this knowledge, one enters the state of unity from that of duality. *Vidyā* does not belong to the realm of the B.A., M.A., or Ph.D., or to science or psychology. When a seeker develops the feeling that the groups of letters are not different from him but are in fact his own body, he experiences the entire universe pulsating in unity with the awareness of *Pūrno'ham* — "I am perfect." The pulsation of "I am the entire universe" is the awareness of *Pūrno'ham*. The Upanishads and other scriptures also call it the potency and secret of the mantra.

266. One who attains the potency of the mantra naturally gains some limited supernatural powers. If he becomes infatuated with them, he fails to pursue the pure knowledge of the Truth, the all-pervasive unity. He remains in the state of ignorance and forgets *Pūrno'ham*. Then the sense of duality and various strange thoughts arise along with his new world of supernatural powers and miracles. It becomes very difficult to escape from this world of miraculous powers. They are a great obstacle to one who wants to attain the all-pervasive unity.

267. Although a seeker may attain limited supernatural powers, he will make further progress only if he rejects these powers as worthless. Such understanding arises through the grace of

---

37. *Shiva Sūtras*, II-2.

God and the Guru. In this way, he will experience the bliss of his own Self in the space of Consciousness. Shaivism calls this awakening of supreme bliss *mantra vīrya*, the power of mantra, or *mudrā vīrya*, the power behind Self-realization.

268.   The grace of Shri Guru is the means of attaining the potency of the mantra. Here, "Guru" refers to the fifth of the five actions of God, that of grace bestowal. The Shakti comes from a Siddha Guru. Grace may be bestowed by a living Siddha or by one who is no longer in the physical body.

269.   The Guru's grace is called *shaktipāt*. Through the power of the unfolding Shakti, a seeker loses the sense of duality which arises from the groups of letters. He experiences the potency of the mantra, which is all-pervasive unity. To one who understands the principle of *mātrikā*, Parashakti gives worldly enjoyment as well as liberation. But when one fails to understand this principle, the *mātrikā shakti*, appearing as subjects and objects, gives rise to joy, sorrow, fear, jealousy, enmity, agitation, and envy. It makes one undergo worldly experiences. One who knows the secret of the *mātrikā shakti* merges the gross and subtle universes into Consciousness. Such a seeker is without pride. His ego and pride have been burned in the fire of knowledge, and only the awareness of *Shivo'ham* — "I am Shiva" — remains.

270.   The knowledge of his own true nature is the source of a yogi's contentment. One of the *Shiva Sūtras* is *Jnānam annam*[38] — "Knowledge is food." Just as contentment is derived from food, it also comes from knowledge. However, knowledge other than that of the Self is mediocre. Another

---

38. Ibid., II-9.

sūtra is *Vismayo yogabhūmikaha*[39] — "The stages of yoga are filled with amazing phenomena." Although there are countless stages of yoga, the scriptural authors emphasized 112. The knowledge of them fills one with amazement.

271. Because a seeker may obtain supernatural powers when he attains the knowledge of his own true nature, he should constantly be vigilant. If he forgets his own Self through ego, he ultimately brings about his downfall. I have seen this happen with many people. These days many ashrams and gurus are falling. The reason for this is partial knowledge and licentiousness. Through the use of intoxicants, things happen which should not happen. Therefore, one should be very careful about choosing a guru or guide. A seeker should not have blind faith.

The purity of a guru should always uplift his disciples. Some people become gurus, teach 108 different therapies, and lead a completely wanton life, without self-control or discipline. A seeker should evaluate such teachers. How can the spiritual path become a haven for therapies? An incomplete teacher who is pure and ethical and who puts his knowledge into practice is far better than an undisciplined person who poses as a perfect guru.

272. Through dualistic knowledge, one becomes infatuated with supernatural powers. Therefore, one should always be careful; one should always contemplate the all-pervasive unity.

273. The *shākta upāya* is a means of transcending worldly existence. It is a technique for pursuing a particular mental awareness arising from the groups of syllables. Groups of

---

39. Ibid., I-12.

syllables contain letters, words, and sentences and are forever
ready to conceal a seeker's true nature. Opinions and thoughts
arise from groups of letters; attachment and aversion spring
from groups of thoughts. But thoughts can also lead to the
thought-free state.

274. Limitless powers are created by groups of letters. Bondage
is the failure to realize the influence of the *shakti chakra*, the
powers of the groups of letters. To understand the powers of
the letters is to attain everything. When one contemplates
and understands isolated thoughts and makes an effort to
pursue unity, this *upāya* is known as the *jnāna upāya*. When
one knows the mighty power which is nondual and the basis
of all thought, whether good or bad, this *upāya* is known as
the *shākta upāya*. Through the means of dualistic knowledge,
knowledge of unity is attained. For that reason, this means is
also called *bhedābheda upāya*, the dual/nondual means.

275. Parāshakti cannot be revealed by articulated speech, but
She can be seen as a result of one-pointed contemplation and
experienced through the oneness brought about by the *shākta
upāya*. This union or absorption comes as a result of pursuing
Her.

> *Ucchārarahitam vastu chetasaiva vichintayan,*
> *Yam samāveshamāpnoti shāktah so'trābhidīyate.* [40]

> When a seeker becomes totally absorbed in the true
> Principle, which is beyond both subtle and articulated
> speech, that oneness is called *shākta samāvesha* or
> *shākta upāya*.

The *shākta upāya* is the process by which the mind and
intellect completely merge into the inner Self.

---

40. *Mālinī Vijaya Tantra.*

276. This section discusses the contemplation of the Supreme Principle; the pursuit of inner unity; the oneness of the mantra, the deity of the mantra, and the seeker; the effort made to unfold one's essential nature; the potency and secret of the mantra; the limited supernatural powers which arise spontaneously along with the obstacles which they create; the bliss of *samādhi* which arises by the rejection of those powers; the nature of this *upāya*; the knowledge of the *mātrikā chakra*; the pursuit of knowledge of the nature of the universe; the contemplation and knowledge of one's own true nature; and the crisis a person goes through if he is not vigilant after attaining supernatural powers. The *shākta upāya* enables a person to become one with the Truth.

277. The discussion of Shaivism always brings joy. By granting the knowledge of the Self, Shaivism destroys ignorance. It takes one across the ocean of the world in the boat of equality.

12

Āṇava Upāya

278. The third section of the *Shiva Sūtras*, on the *āṇava upāya*, is longer than the sections on both the *shāmbhava upāya* and the *shākta upāya* combined. In addition, the *āṇava upāya* has a specific quality: Everyone can follow this path. Some portions of it resemble the *shākta upāya*. By following the *āṇava upāya*, a seeker progresses gradually. The section dealing with *āṇava upāya* consists of forty-five *sūtras*. It is lengthy so that ordinary people will be able to understand this *upāya*.

> *Ucchāra karana dhyāna varna sthāna prakalpanaihi,*
> *Yo bhavettu samāveshaha samyagānava ucchyate.*[41]

> In *āṇava upāya*, the perfect absorption into the essential divine Self is achieved through methods known as *ucchāra*, *karana*, *dhyāna*, *varna*, and *sthānakalpanā*.

Ucchāra is the stilling of the *prāna* through the practice of So'ham mantra. By stilling the *prāna* through various means, one experiences different kinds of bliss: *nijānanda*, the bliss of one's own Self; *nirānanda*, transcendental bliss; *parānanda*,

---

41. Ibid.

supreme bliss; *brahmananda*, the bliss of the Absolute; *mahānanda*, great bliss; *chidānanda*, the bliss of Consciousness; *jagadānanda*, the bliss of the world. All these are included within *ucchāra*. Among all the types of *prānāyāma*, the natural one is *So'ham*. It is the greatest centering technique; through it comes the complete attainment of *pūrnānanda*, perfect bliss.

Karana is the practice of contemplating the subtle and gross bodies as a replica of the cosmos. This is possible only through *shaktipāt*.

Varna refers to *nādānusandhana*, the hearing of divine sounds when the *prāna* is retained in the *sahasrāra*, or crown of the head. Yogis experience ten different divine sounds. This is possible only through *dhyāna* (meditation).

Sthānakalpanā refers to centering the mind on the breath, the body, or objects outside the body. The highest centering technique is the awareness that whatever exists in this world is a play of the Universal Consciousness.

279. A being who has become all-pervasive is not limited by birth and death, pain and pleasure, the endless rounds of incarnation in different planes, or the agitation caused by changes. However, one who has given up his all-pervasive nature and become limited undergoes pain and affliction. As long as he remains limited, this will continue to happen. Pain and affliction are experienced through the body and senses, which are subject to the three *gunas*, *sattva*, *rajas*, and *tamas*. This kind of experience is bondage and is the source of sorrow and dryness. A bound individual does not fully understand the body, *prāna*, or senses, through which he undergoes pain and pleasure. In other words, he lacks the knowledge of his own Self. He sees no difference between his true nature and pain and pleasure. This is ignorance, bondage, and lack of discrimination.

280. The physical body, which is made of the five elements, should be fully understood; so should the *puryashtaka*, or subtle body, which is composed of the five *tanmatras*, or rudimentary elements, along with the mind, ego, and intellect. One should also understand the gross and subtle principles from Shiva to the earth.

Everyone experiences one object as different from another. However, by understanding the Guru's instructions and by contemplation, one comes to perceive unity in duality. As one's knowledge evolves and one's *sādhanā* matures, one experiences the state of unity. In the same way, one should meditate and merge the mundane and supramundane paths, called *bhuvana adhvā*, *tattva adhvā*, *kalā adhvā*, and so on, with pure Consciousness.[42] This is the way to become free from bondage.

These techniques bring about supernatural powers, such as *nādī-samhāra* (dissolution of the *prāna* flowing through the nasal passages), *bhūta-jaya* (control of the elements), *bhūta-kaivalya* (withdrawal of the mind from the elements), and *bhūta-prithaktva* (separation from the elements).

In *nādī-samhāra*, the *nādīs* referred to are the passages through which the inbreath and the outbreath pass. Through the natural yoga of So'ham, *prānāyāma* spontaneously takes place, the *nādīs* are purified within, and the *sushumnā* unfolds. Through *prānāyāma*, the *prāna* becomes still in the inner *dvādashānta* (the space located at a distance of twelve fingers from the tip of the nose, where the breath merges in the heart) and the outer *dvādashānta* (the point located at a distance of twelve fingers from the tip of the nose, where the breath merges outside). In this way, one becomes centered.

By the centering technique of *bhūta-jaya*, one attains mastery over the elements. *Bhūta-kaivalya* comes about when, as

---

42. See Glossary for *bhuvana adhvā*, etc.

a result of *shaktipāt*, the *prāna* becomes still in the heart during meditation. The *prāna* is controlled by the mind. When the mind turns away from sensory stimuli and stabilizes in the navel, it becomes quiet. This is called the power of withdrawal of the mind from objects.

In *bhūta-prithaktva*, one should become separate from all the elements, and the tendencies of the mind should become still. As a yogi experiences both of these, he transcends all tendencies and attains the freedom of his own true nature. In this way, by eliminating ignorance, he attains *sahajavidya*, the natural awareness which roots out all the impressions left by the supernatural powers. *Sahajavidyā* and *shuddhavidyā*, pure awareness, are one and the same.

According to Shaivism, the universe is the form of Shakti, the Supreme Principle. Shiva and Shakti are one; they are not separate. A yogi who has attained *sahajavidyā* considers the universe to be the light of his own Self, like the light produced by a flame. The knowledge of one's own true nature (*aham*, "I") and the knowledge of the universe (*idam*, "this") merge into all-pervasive unity. This is the understanding that one should have. The knowledge of "I" is like a flame, and the knowledge of "this" is like its light, which spreads everywhere equally.

A seeker in whom the knowledge of the Self is strong performs all his various actions in the realm of duality like an actor or an actress who displays different feelings and emotions in a play. Just as these limited feelings and expressions are reserved for the stage, so this individual's state of bondage is simply a limitation of his true nature. The senses are the audience, but the knowledge of the Truth is his understanding of the play. Through the vibration of his senses, he performs in the drama of the world, which is filled with mundane activities.

When he feels that he is an individual, he is limited like an actor in a play. When he attains the all-pervasive unity through the evolution of his knowledge into *sahajavidyā*, he becomes independent. But even when he becomes free, he should continually meditate on Parashakti, which ceaselessly vibrates and which is the source of the universe. Through the power of the touch of a *shākta* (one who possesses Shakti), he is infused with bliss. From this, he directly experiences the state of Shiva, the awareness of Shiva, and the manifest Self.

281.   If the knowledge of *sahajavidyā* has not been tainted, there can be no rebirth. *Sahajavidyā* is an understanding. Just as there is the understanding "I am the body," so *sahajavidyā* is the spontaneous and effortless awareness "I am Paramashiva." Even after a seeker experiences the state of *sahajavidyā*, if he fails to maintain that awareness, he becomes bound once again. If a seeker acquires a bit of verbal knowledge and then gives up his *sādhanā* to become a guru, this brings misfortune.

The Goddess Parashakti first takes the forms of *icchā shakti*, *jnāna shakti*, and *kriyā shakti*, the powers of will, knowledge, and action. Then She undergoes a transformation and becomes vowels, consonants, and classified and unclassified letters. The Shakti, becoming *mātrikā*, takes the form of the letters from *a* to *ksha*, giving rise to positive and negative feelings. Through its power, this newborn *shakti* conceals the unity of Self-awareness. Then it gives rise to its friends — attachment, aversion, desire, and craving for sense pleasures — and alters a seeker's direction. While deluding the seeker into feeling that he is being led along a true path to the perfect bliss of the Self, it takes him to the limited bliss of sense pleasures. It guides seekers, gurus, *bhagawāns*, and many others in the wrong direction. That is why, even after a seeker attains Siddhahood, he should be vigilant and always remain in *sahajavidyā*.

A person should make his contemplation of the *turīya* state permeate his waking, dream, and deep sleep states like oil spreading over water. He should transcend the breathing process of inhalation and exhalation and all other external manifestations and become absorbed in the knowledge of the Supreme Principle. He should maintain equal vision in the face of all duality, whether internal or external. To see equality everywhere is the outlook of Shiva.

282. When a seeker is trying to attain the *turīya* state, the tendency to perceive duality arises from time to time because of his old impressions and desires. He should assimilate all these impressions through practice of the awareness of the unity to be attained in the *turīya* state. When he does that, *Shiva-tulyo jāyate*[43] — "He becomes like Shiva." Then he is Shiva while in the body and after leaving the body.

As long as a person is in the body, he should pursue his own true nature as resolutely as if he were observing a vow. A firm vow is never broken under any circumstances. The moment he fulfills his staunch vow of *sahajavidyā*, he becomes like Shiva. Then everything he says is mantra repetition. Whatever he gives is knowledge of the Self. Such a person can awaken knowledge in others with his own power. He sees the world as the play of his own Shakti. For him, creation, sustenance, and dissolution are like the blinking of an eye. Although he pursues the supreme "I"-consciousness of the *turīya* state, he rejects neither the worldly nor the spiritual life. For him, *Sarvam shivamayam jagat* — "The world is the embodiment of Shiva."

283. A seeker who pursues the knowledge of the perfect "I"-consciousness through the *ānava upāya* becomes one with

---

43. *Shiva Sūtras*, III-25.

the Supreme Consciousness and considers pain and pleasure to be separate from him. He feels that the pain he undergoes does not belong to him. If he has this kind of detachment, he becomes established in his real Self. If he fails to achieve this, he becomes the embodiment of delusion, involved in good and bad deeds.

Through the power of *sādhanā*, a seeker experiences pure knowledge. He attains the power to form a new creation. What is night for an owl is day for a crow. That which is a mere world for a materialistic person is Kailāsa, the abode of God, for a Shiva yogi. For him, everything becomes the embodiment of Shiva. Through the power of his knowledge of the Truth, he gives a new direction to the world.

284. A yogi who follows the *āṇava upāya* takes delight in the creation, sustenance, and dissolution of the universe. He can manipulate his body, mind, and senses as he pleases. His limited identification as an individual dissolves. Although he has a physical body, he is equal to Shiva. With his own free power of will, he remains in contact with his *prāna shakti*, the vital force, and other powers. He needs no other *sādhanā*. His primary nature is the knowledge of Consciousness.

285. The third section of the *Shiva Sūtras* describes the limited condition of the bound soul, bondage, *māyā*, delusion, the sheaths or coverings of the individual soul, and *sahajavidyā*, the spontaneous awareness. It also discusses the detachment of the individual soul, his relationship with the senses, his awareness of freedom, the state of *samādhi*, and the cessation of rebirth. In addition, it deals with the bondage which arises from the letters of the alphabet as well as with the *turīya* state, which is its opposite. It explains the intermediate stage which exists as long as a seeker's bondage has not yet been

completely eradicated and discusses how Siddhahood makes him equal to Shiva.

As long as a Siddha lives, his presence offers infinite benefit to the world. In this world, such a great being is a haven of peace for tormented souls. He is the physician who cures the disease of worldliness. He is the witness of the bliss of knowledge.

286. The excellence of his awareness is extraordinary. Because he is using the elements merely as a covering, he remains equal to the Lord of all beings. *Naisargikaha prānasambandhaha*[44] — "He has a natural link with the *prāna shakti*."

The third section of the *Shiva Sūtras* also explains at length how the *prāna* is separated from the physical body at death.

---

44. Ibid., III-43.

13

A Summary of the Upāyas

287. The *shāmbhava upāya*, which is also known as *icchā upāya* or *abheda upāya*, involves experiencing one's own true nature through *icchā shakti*, or the power of will. This *shakti* is one of the powers of Consciousness, like *jñānā shakti* and *kriyā shakti*. In *shāmbhava upāya*, there is no need for mental or intellectual activity.

The *shākta upāya*, *bhedābheda upāya*, or *jñānā upāya* involves attaining oneness with Shiva by contemplating the thoughts of the mind. One regards the groups of letters which cause these thoughts as nothing other than forms of Shakti, the essence of the universe.

288. The *ānava upāya* is ordinarily called the *bheda upāya*, the dualistic path, but in actuality it is also *abheda upāya*, a nondual path, because it leads to unity. It involves the use of the body, mind, intellect, senses, and *prāna shakti*. By pursuing the knowledge of the Truth through *japa* and meditation, a person becomes one with Shiva and attains peace of mind.

289. So we have come to know something of the three *upāyas*. These means of *sādhanā* help us to realize Shiva.

290. Shiva, the Self of all, has already been attained. These *upāyas* exist not to make us attain the Self, but to remove our forgetfulness, our errors, and our ignorance of that Self. Everyone has already attained the Self but is unaware of it. The way to Self-realization is the recognition of one's own Self as Shiva, and this occurs through the *upāyas*. You are perfect, you have come from perfection, you live in perfection, and this perfection is the Supreme Truth.

291. There is a fourth *upāya*, which is called the *anupāya*. It is sublime, subtle, and profound. This *upāya* is for superior candidates, intense seekers who are fully ripe. In this *upāya*, a seeker's worthiness is paramount, and no actions, rituals, or meditation are needed. Either by simply hearing the Guru's instructions or through scriptural proofs, one immediately and with unshakable faith recognizes the Shiva Principle, and becomes completely firm in it. If one recognizes gold once, one does not have to study it over and over again. It is not difficult to identify it. We do not need to know the scriptures to recognize our parents. Once our mother shows us who our father is, we do not have to meditate on him incessantly or repeat the mantra of his name. We always know him. In the same way, at the precise moment when one recognizes the inner Consciousness as *prakāsha* and *vimarsha*,[45] one becomes perfect. This is the *anupāya* or the *Guru kripā upāya*, the path of Guru's grace. This *upāya* depends on a seeker's worthiness.

---

45. *Prakāsha* and *vimarsha* are the two aspects of Paramashiva. *Prakāsha* is Shiva, the static aspect, which is of the nature of light. *Vimarsha* is the dynamic aspect, or Shakti, through which Paramashiva is able to survey Himself. See Glossary for more details.

14

Paramashiva:
The Supreme Consciousness

292.   Shaivism reveals its essence in the statement *Chaitanyam ātmā*[46] — "The Self is Consciousness." Consciousness is the perfect Principle, which is all-pervasive. Since it is all-pervasive, nothing can be added to it. It lacks nothing, nor does it have an excess of anything. Shiva, who is complete and exists everywhere, is *Chaitanyam ātmā.* Paramashiva is the waveless ocean of Consciousness. Through His play, that serene ocean has become the universe of *grāhaka*, the perceiver, and *grāhya*, the perceived. By becoming the thirty-six *tattvas*,[47] or principles, that Consciousness gives rise to the universe and its activities.

  This universe of ordinary experience contains infinite permutations of Consciousness, such as *nīla, sukha, deha*, and *prāna. Nīla*, the color blue, is among the countless colors and forms that make up the objects perceived through the outer senses. *Sukha*, pleasure, is one of the many experiences of the

---

46. *Shiva Sūtras*, I-1.

47. Shaivism describes thirty-six categories, called *tattvas*, to explain the stages of manifestation of the universe. *Tattva*, which is loosely translated as "principle," means that which is the essence of each stage of manifestation. See Glossary for more details.

inner senses. *Deha,* the body, is the basis of both inner and outer experiences. *Prāna,* the vital force, is one of the many conscious powers that make the body perform actions. In this way, the universe is full of numerous unique forms.

For practical purposes, the universe is divided into four categories: the knower, the means of knowing, the objects known, and knowledge. In scriptural language, these are called *pramātri, pramāna, prameya,* and *pramiti. Pramātri* is the limited, individual soul. He understands the nature and activities of the universe through *pramāna,* the different ways of knowing. Whatever he cannot understand through direct perception, he experiences through the other *pramānas,* such as inference and scriptural authority. The universe is *prameya,* and his right understanding of the universe is *pramiti.*

The experience of the waveless Consciousness does not have these categories. It is Paramashiva, *Chaitanyam ātmā.* Since the universe is not different from Him, there are no means separate from Him by which to know Him. *Upāya jālam na shivam prakāshayet*[48] — "No means can illumine Shiva." Shiva is both the means and the end. Just as a flashlight illumines everything in a darkened room, it also illumines itself. No other light is needed to reveal light; it reveals itself and other objects as well. Similarly, Consciousness reveals its own nature and also gives the knowledge of other objects.

293. Consciousness is both self-luminous and independent. It encompasses all powers and is the cause of everything. It is called Parāsamvit, Paramashiva, and Chaitanya. Paramashiva is as serene as a still ocean. In this state, Shiva is transcendental. He is always filled with bliss. In His immanent aspect, through the independent power of His supreme "I"-

---

48. Abhinavagupta, *Tantrāsāra.*

consciousness, Paramashiva becomes the thirty-six *tattvas*, or principles, and reveals the seven experiencers[49] from within Himself.

294.   Paramashiva, the Self of all, exists as the universe in its infinite forms. It is His play. The five powers — *chit, ānanda, icchā, jñāna,* and *kriyā* — continually dwell in Him, whether He is in His transcendental or His immanent aspect. Through His power of illumination, *chit shakti,* Paramashiva is self-luminous and wholly independent. Through *ānanda shakti,* He has the ability to experience bliss within Himself without any external cause; He is the embodiment of supreme bliss. Because of *icchā shakti,* His willpower, He can do anything in a miraculous way without opposition and with firm resolution. Through His power of knowledge, *jñāna shakti,* He can assimilate into Himself both the perceiver and the perceived. With His power of action, *kriyā shakti,* He can create objects of various forms.

With these five powers, He continually performs five actions: creation, sustenance, dissolution, concealment, and bestowal of grace. Creation refers to the creation of the universe. Sustenance means the maintenance of this creation. Dissolution is the absorption of the creation into Himself. Concealment is the state in which the creation remains within Him in a potential form before being remembered or re-created. Bestowal of grace refers to the complete merging of the creation into the Universal Consciousness, or Chiti, eradicating all impressions and all opportunities for subsequent remembrance.

---

49. The names given to the experiencer at different levels of consciousness. The seven experiencers begin with Shiva at the highest level and descend to the *sakala* (bound individual soul) at the lowest level.

In this way, Paramashiva is complete and independent and possesses five powers and five actions. He is both transcendent and immanent, the totality of the bliss of Consciousness, the constant Knower. Paramashiva is self-luminous and is the root cause of the universe. Out of His own being, He manifests this universe full of multiplicity and countless forms, yet remains the embodiment of Consciousness. He is the foundation of the world. Although the manifold universe issues forth from Shiva, His true nature undergoes no change. It neither decreases nor increases. He is supremely pure.

15

God's Independent and Inseparable Shakti

295. Just as gentle waves arise on the surface of the ocean, a throb or movement arises in the ocean of Consciousness, and this throb is called Shakti or Chitshakti. This same Shakti expands in three forms: *icchā*, *jnāna*, and *kriyā*. That first movement in Consciousness is called *spanda, sphurattā,* or *unmesha*. From this initial throb comes the creation of the cosmos, in which Shakti becomes the thirty-six *tattvas*, the principles from Shiva to the earth. There is no difference between the two *tattvas* of Shiva and Shakti, nor is there any difference between the perceiver and the perceived. In the context of the thirty-six principles, Shiva is considered the first principle. *Icchā, jnāna,* and *kriyā* manifest from the Shakti, or second principle. The perceiver and the perceived originate in the third principle, Sadāshiva. The various classes of the perceived come into existence from the other principles of creation. The three *shaktis, icchā, jnāna,* and *kriyā*, become the universe and encompass all duality.

  The miracle of Chitshakti is Her extraordinary activity of revealing the universe of the perceiver and the perceived and then reabsorbing it into Herself. Chitshakti is uniquely independent. She reabsorbs the outer universe and can manifest it in countless ways whenever She desires. Chitshakti is astonishing. She can accomplish anything and become anything. She is also known as Kundalinī. She is the Siddha Yoginī who performs actions spontaneously. She is the grace-bestowing power of God, which resides in the Guru. She makes inner *kriyās* take place. She pervades everyone in the world equally but remains pure and different from all. She is called Shive. Her blessing is the perpetual and sublime bliss of the yogis. In the form of this supreme bliss, She dwells in the hearts of all as the Self.

Chitshakti has no limitations of space, time, or object. However, the universe that arises from Her has those limitations, which make it possible for all activities to go on within it. Although this is so, the universe is still not different from Shiva. The world is the embodiment of Shiva.

296. In order to complete the task of the all-encompassing expansion of the universe of sound and matter, the currents of the same Parameshwarī Shakti keep expanding in forms such as *mātrikās*; the presiding deities of the eight classes of letters, namely, Yogīshwarī, Brāhmī, Māheshwarī, Vaishnavī, Vārāhī, Aindrī, Kaumārī, and Chāmundā; and the *shaktis* which preside over the inner psychic instruments and the outer sense organs, namely, Bhūcharī, Dikcharī, and Gocharī. Then She flows out as the *prāna*, the intellect, the four psychic instruments,[50] the five senses of perception,[51] the five powers of action, and all the elements.[52]

The point of stating this is to emphasize that all the countless objects of the universe from Brahmā to a blade of

---

50. Mind, subconscious mind, intellect, and ego.
51. Seeing, hearing, touching, tasting, and smelling.
52. Ether, air, fire, water, and earth.

grass, which are manifest and subject to experience, are nothing but Shiva. The world is the embodiment of Shiva. All these forms are streams of the infinite Shakti of the Supreme. The scriptural name for these limitless currents of Shakti is the *shakti chakra*. The *shakti chakra* is full of glory. This glory of the Lord is the sign of His independent power to create or not create anything or to change anything.

16

Ābhāsavāda:
The Theory of Manifestation

297.   The self-luminous Paramashiva is the cause of the universe. He is the embodiment of Consciousness, the substratum of all. Out of His own being, He has manifested this universe filled with multiplicity. But although the universe issues forth from Shiva, His true nature does not undergo any change. It neither decreases nor increases. In Shaivism, this process of manifestation is discussed according to *ābhāsavāda*, or the theory of manifestation.

   The root of the word *ābhāsa* is *bhā*, which means *dīptau*, to shine forth. Whether one has an actual object or simply the knowledge of an object, both come into existence in the perfection of their own individuality through the process of manifestation called *ābhāsa*.

   Under *ābhāsavāda*, two points are discussed: first, how the experience of our inner world is transformed into the experience of the outer world, and second, the objects which we experience in the external world. For example, when we want an object, we obtain it by saying its name. In this way, our inner experience changes into the actual outer experience of the object. Similarly, the universe consists of many *ābhāsas*, or manifestations, of Shiva, both within and with-

105

out. The nature of Shiva neither gains nor loses anything from these *ābhāsas*. Moreover, they remain separate from each other although they are one in Him.

298. Even without concerning ourselves with outer objects, we can understand the subject of *ābhāsas* by examining our own inner experience. Our understandings arise from one another. So many of our understandings of different things lie hidden, to be revealed when they are triggered by events or thoughts. We say, "I saw, I heard, I knew," and thus the "I"-principle always remains one with our experience. It never becomes separate from it. All our understandings branch out with this "I"-principle as their basis. These different understandings, which come and go, are our *ābhāsas*, our manifestations. But no matter how many thoughts arise, the "I"-principle does not change. It neither increases nor decreases.

299. In the *ābhāsavāda*, the theory of manifestation, we discover another extraordinary fact. In our understanding of even one object, there are many *ābhāsas*. Sometimes we perceive an object as one unit but simultaneously see it as having many different aspects. We are perceiving the "concealed" aspects of that object. For example, suppose that someone is looking at a book. If he does not think much about it, he simply considers it to be a book. This is the *vishishtha ābhāsa*, its generalized or unified manifestation. Then he perceives the different aspects of the book — its subject matter, print, language, the reason why he is reading it, and so on. These are all different *ābhāsas*. From a nondual viewpoint, he sees the book as a book, but from an analytical viewpoint, he sees it as being composed of different parts.

In all our activities, we perceive an object from one point of view as a unit and from another point of view as being composed of differences. In this way, every object appears as both unity and diversity. No matter how many contradictions or dissimilarities an object may contain, they do not interfere with our overall understanding of that object. Similarly, an outer object, the understanding of that object, the understanding which comes from language, the knowledge of the empirical world, and the knowledge which lies beyond the realm of the senses are all *ābhāsas*. These *ābhāsas* exist in the outer world and in the experience of the inner world, without intermingling. They always remain individual and separate from each other. No matter how complex or different these *ābhāsas* may be, the "I"-principle is not altered. It neither gains nor loses anything.

In this way, although Shiva manifests the universe in multiplicity, His true nature is unchanging. He always remains complete. The universe is Shiva's *ābhāsa*, just as all the things that we understand are our *ābhāsas*. The *ābhāsavada* is an important concept in Shaivism.

300.   We describe an object by saying, "This is of a certain type." "This" indicates its nature; "a certain type" indicates its qualities. For example, imagine that there is an object lying on a table. First we see it as *idam*, "this." Then we see its qualities and nature, and we say, "This is a pencil." Although the qualities and names may vary, "this-ness" is common to all things. Shiva pervades all the activities of the universe as *idam*. The universe is His *ābhāsa*. All the new things that appear are revealed by His *chit shakti*. The great being Utpālachārya said in the *Ishwara Pratyabhijnā* that whatever exists in this world is Shiva's *ābhāsa*.

17

Bimba Pratibimba Nyāya: The Theory of an Object and Its Reflection

301. *Nirmale mukure yadvad bhānti bhūmijalādayaha,*
    Āmishrās tadvad ekasmin chinmātre vishva vrittayaha. [53]

    Just as earth, water, and so on, are reflected in a clear
    mirror without intermingling, in the same way the
    entire world is reflected in one God, the embodi-
    ment of Consciousness.

    Everything in the universe is reflected in pure Chiti, yet all
    these objects always remain separate from each other.

302. A reflection appears in a mirror or on a clear surface. The
    mirror and the object reflected in it are different from each
    other, although they do not appear to be so. Even if a large
    object is reflected in a small mirror, the mirror does not
    undergo any change; its size remains the same. Moreover,
    even if many objects are reflected in a mirror, they do not
    intermingle with one another. For example, even though fire
    and cotton may be reflected simultaneously in the same
    mirror, the cotton in the mirror does not burn. When a cow

---

53. Abhinavagupta, *Tantrāloka.*

and a tiger are reflected in a mirror, the cow is not afraid of the tiger and the tiger does not attack the cow. Since only the forms of objects are seen in the mirror, they do not intermingle with one another. Moreover, in order for there to be a reflection, the reflecting surface must be clear. The clearer the surface is, the clearer the reflection will be.

303. There is another requirement. If something is to be reflected, there must be an object, and that object must have a form. Formless space cannot be reflected.

304. As was mentioned earlier, wherever there is clarity, an object can be reflected. We see our face in a mirror, but we cannot see the mirror in our face. Therefore, we can say that the face lacks the clarity to reflect. This is an analogy of the relationship between the external world and God: God reveals the world, but the world cannot reveal God. Of course, the clearer a surface is, the brighter the reflection will be. In the same way, the clearer our heart becomes, the brighter will be the reflection of Shiva.

305. The world which we experience is a conglomeration of five elements. The human body is a microcosm composed of these five elements, and all the objects of the world have sprung from them. The five elements have five qualities: sound, touch, form, taste, and smell. Every material object has these five qualities. A person has five senses to perceive and reflect the corresponding qualities. Sound is reflected in the ears, touch in the skin, form in the eyes, taste in the tongue, and smell in the nose. However, the senses do not have the power to perceive them independently. For this, the senses need the help of the four psychic instruments as well as of Chiti Shakti. As the strength of the senses is

increased, objects are reflected and perceived more clearly and in finer detail. People who have expanded their sensory capacity and the depth of their feeling through *sādhanā* have sharper and clearer sense perception than most people. Such beings are called yogis.

306.   The entire universe is concealed in the supreme space of God. Similarly, all tendencies born of the senses are hidden in the space of an individual's consciousness. The principle of *bimba pratibimba* — an object and its reflection — holds true for God as well as for a human being and his sense perceptions.

There is another point of interest: When we use the analogy of an object and its reflection, we speak of a mirror as the basis for the reflection. That which is being reflected is separate from the mirror, but when it is seen, it is called a reflection. So three things are involved: an object, its reflection, and a mirror. However, the principle of an object and its reflection is different when applied to God and the universe. In this case, there are not three separate entities. Shiva, or Consciousness, is all three — the object, the reflecting instrument, and the reflection. Shiva is the object, and the world is His reflection.

307.   Because a crystal is completely clear, it can reflect anything anywhere. Similarly, since Consciousness is eternally pure, it has the ability to reflect forms, tastes, and so on. It can also reflect the specific qualities of objects, such as heaviness or lightness. This reflection happens both internally and externally. When external objects are reflected through the senses, we become either happy or unhappy. When we remember something from within, we also experience either happiness or unhappiness. When something is reflected through the outer senses, the sensory perception

produces a subtle vibration. In the same way, the happiness or unhappiness arising within produces a vibration. This inner vibration is *prakāsha* and *vimarsha*. If there is no vibration in our physical body or in our feelings, there can be no inner experience.

308. The pain and pleasure which arise in our lives are experienced in two ways. They may arise either through inner remembrance or through the perception of outer objects. The latter occurs when the senses come in contact with their objects. If we think about the pain and pleasure which arise in these two ways, we realize that they occur because of the vibration produced by our sensory perception.

Pain and pleasure are reflections of some of the five qualities of the elements. These reflections cause a vibration in our sensory perception, which in turn produces involvements such as anger and desire. This is our experience. Once the tendencies which arise in this way merge back into Chiti, there is no longer any experience of pain or pleasure. To experience them anew, we have to remember them or once again be in contact with external objects. An enlightened being does not become attached to momentary pain or pleasure. He realizes that they are merely reflections. The *Bhagavad Gītā* says:

> *Mātrā sparshāstu kaunteya shītoshna sukha duhkhadāhā,*
> *Āgamāpāyino'nityās tāmstitikshasva bhārata.* [54]
>
> O son of Kunti, the contacts of the senses with their objects, which cause heat and cold, pleasure and pain, have a beginning and an end. They are impermanent. Endure them bravely, O Arjuna.

---

54. *Bhagavad Gītā*, II-14.

As long as the senses are not in contact with external objects, we do not experience pleasure or pain. Even if they come in contact with their objects, we experience neither pleasure nor pain if the perception and the experience merge into Chiti. However, in the intermediate stage before the perception merges into Chiti, we still experience pleasure or pain.

309. By understanding the principle of *bimba pratibimba*, the object and its reflection, we understand the true nature of pain and pleasure and attain peace.

310. Everything that we know is simply a reflection. Whether it is an inner experience or the perception of outer objects, it cannot be anything other than a reflection. By contemplating these reflections, which are the source of duality, we understand the difference between them and the experience of our own true nature, which leads to all-pervasive unity. The understanding of the principle of *bimba pratibimba* is very helpful in attaining this experience. Through it, we learn to reject reflections, which are the cause of pain. When we have firm faith that the universe is reflected in Chiti, our attachment and aversion disappear into Consciousness. Then we attain the bliss of Consciousness.

311. *Bimba pratibimba* is one of the most beautiful principles of Shaivism. The universe is a reflection in Paramashiva, who is Satchidānanda. *Bimba* is *pratibimba*; the object and its reflection are identical. Shiva is in the world and the world is in Shiva. Shiva and the world are not two but one. The principle of *bimba pratibimba* is true knowledge. We have already attained Shivahood and Shiva Himself. The Shaiva philosophy is concerned with how to make this experience manifest.

18

The Kingdom of Vikalpa

312. *Vividha kalpaha vikalpaha; vikalpas* are various kinds of thoughts and fantasies. We have various kinds of understanding. Moreover, each kind of understanding is a complete unit within itself. In technical language, the different kinds of understanding are called *vikalpas*. These mental constructs have innumerable progeny, which take birth and then die instantly. All the various understandings of the principles from Shiva to the earth are *vikalpas*. Without duality, there is no *vikalpa*. Duality is the birthplace of *vikalpa*.

   Dvitiyād vai bhayam bhavati — "Fear arises because of duality." The Upanishads say that to harbor the idea of "others" is to experience fear. All ideas such as "I and mine," "his and theirs," and "I am different from others" exist because of the power of *vikalpa*. If there is no thought in one's mental world, that state is called *nirvikalpa*, or thought-free.

   Svānūbhuti rasāveshād drishya shabdāvupekshya tu,
   Nirvikalpah samādhih syān nivātasthaladīpavat.[55]

---

55. Shankarāchārya, *Vākyasudhā*, 26.

> When a seeker experiences the bliss of his own true
> nature, he ignores what is seen and heard and stills
> his mind like a flame where there is no wind. This is
> called *nirvikalpa samādhi.*

Learned men say that any state which is still confined within
space, time, and object is classified as *vikalpa.* A state that is
free of these things is *nirvikalpa.* Because of the current of
vikalpa, Shakti contracts and bondage comes into existence.
In this state, the power of *vikalpa* is the cause of pain and
pleasure, attachment and aversion. Because *vikalpa* is incred-
ibly powerful, it is the cause of limitless complications. One
can count external objects, but one cannot count *vikalpas.*
From one *vikalpa* arises another of the same kind. Many
vikalpas frequently arise from one, and one *vikalpa* arises from
many. The offspring of *vikalpas* are extraordinary. Just as
their growth is amazing, so is their destruction. A *vikalpa* is
destroyed either by an opposite *vikalpa* or by fading away. In
other words, one *vikalpa* can arise from another and undergo
many modifications, or else that *vikalpa* can become *nirvikalpa.*

313. To understand *vikalpas,* we can categorize them into four
      groups: those in an unmanifest state, those which are begin-
      ning to manifest, those which are at the point of fully
      manifesting, and those which are fully manifest. *Vikalpas* in
      the last three stages give rise to pleasure and pain.

314. When even ordinary people spend time in the company of
      the great, they too become great. If they keep bad company,
      they are corrupted. Just as *vikalpas* can be affected by one's
      interactions in the outer world, similarly, in a subtle way and
      with even greater intensity, *vikalpas* can undergo change
      within.

315.   The current of *vikalpas* is astonishing and flows incessantly. But sometimes in the midst of it, like a flash of lightning, there occurs an instant which is free of *vikalpas*. In that instant, there is contact with Consciousness. This is the state of one's true nature.

316.   While one is reading or running, or experiencing fear, happiness, or surprise, or pronouncing particular vowel sounds called *visargas*, there may be a moment when everything is suspended, when one can neither understand nor say anything. At this moment, one experiences a state without thought-waves. The *upāyas* were created to stabilize this thought-free state.

It has already been stated that the different kinds of understanding of the principles from Shiva to the earth are *vikalpas*. For convenience and practicality, we can describe these *vikalpas* in three ways. The first group of *vikalpas* enables us to carry on our mundane life in the world. The second group helps us to attain our true nature by enabling us to understand the principles of *parā* (*abheda*, the supreme nonduality), *parāparā* (*bhedābheda*, unity in diversity), and *aparā* (*bheda*, duality). The third group is used to remove one by one the progeny of the other *vikalpas* and to attain the thought-free state.

Although there is no *vikalpa* which is different from Shiva, the *vikalpas* arise through ignorance. We should root out all the *vikalpas* which lead us to believe that worldly objects are different from one another. We pursue the *nirvikalpa* state to attain our true nature, which is self-luminous and untainted by ignorance. The *vikalpas* that we use to eradicate the *vikalpas* of duality destroy these *vikalpas* and disappear. Then only the *samvit* state, the state of pure Consciousness, remains. This is the state of the blissful Self. We can neither remove anything from Consciousness nor add anything to it. Our goal is to experience Consciousness.

Of course, all the efforts which are made to escape the tumult of the *vikalpas* are also *vikalpas*. But they are *vikalpas* of *shuddhavidyā*, or pure knowledge. The *vikalpas* which cause suffering pertain to *ashuddhavidyā*, or impure knowledge. A person who is infatuated with impure *vikalpas* — ignorance of his own true nature, a negative attitude toward the Self, lack of faith in God, striving to acquire material objects, indifference toward turning within — repents his whole life long. To acquire pure *vikalpas* and make them constantly arise within us, we should receive the Sadguru's instructions, practice *sādhanā*, keep good company, and engage in uplifting conversation. Even through such conversation, a seeker can decide, according to his understanding, how to expand to his true nature. If a person follows some practice, such as continually contemplating a flame, he can have a direct realization of the Truth. Through the power of that realization, there arises in him the awareness "I am transcendent as well as immanent. *Pūrno'ham* — I am perfect."

One who merely reads a book about the *Pūrno'ham* awareness can only gossip about it. He cannot become *Pūrno'ham*. How can dry knowledge make one juicy? In the world, there are many book-*jñānis*.[56]

There is a saying: "A scholar is like a torch." A torch has an oily rag tied to one end. This rag is set on fire, and a person carries it at night to illumine his path. Although the torch gives light to all, the area beneath the flame remains in darkness. In the same way, a scholar gives one lecture after another but fails to understand their essence himself. For that reason, the Guru's guidance, good company, the practice of *sādhanā*, and discussion of the Truth are absolutely necessary. By these means, a seeker easily attains his own true nature, the all-pervasive and perfect "I"-consciousness, and merges with the Truth. Perfection merges with perfection.

---

56. *Jñāni:* a knower of the Truth.

317. In the state of bondage, the mind is the basis of all *vikalpas*. In the *Yoga Sūtras*, Patanjali says, *Yogash chitta-vritti-nirodhaha*[57] — "Yoga is the inhibition of the modifications of the mind." It is everyone's experience that the journey of life is made through the *vikalpas* arising in the mind. Through withdrawal of the senses, concentration, meditation, and other spiritual practices, the *vikalpas* should be roasted. If *vikalpas* arise even after one is pursuing one's own true nature, their strength should be reduced.

Two main points are discussed in the *shākta upāya*: how to use the *vikalpas* in a positive way in order to become free of them and how to become established in the *nirvikalpa* state. The practices which we use to make the *vikalpas* positive belong to the realm of duality, but the practices which we use to become established in the *nirvikalpa* state lead to the vision of unity. These practices are also known as *jnāna upāya*. A great being who has attained realization through this *upāya* experiences the bliss of God and the nectar of the totality of Consciousness. He experiences them at all times, while awake, asleep, at work, at home, in the market, and in the factory.

> *Yatra yatra manas tushtir manas tatraiva dhārayet,*
> *Tatra tatra parānanda svarūpam sampravartate.*[58]

> Wherever a person's mind finds satisfaction, let it concentrate on that. In every such case, the true nature of the highest bliss will manifest.

The satisfaction of the mind lies in joy, not in agitation. If a yogi does not control his mind, it becomes agitated by the various *vikalpas* and makes him fall from his yogic state. Only by quieting the agitation of desire, anger, and so on, can the

---

57. *Patanjali Yoga Sūtras*, I-2.
58. *Vijnāna Bhairava*, 74.

yogi still his mind. Therefore, he should practice making the mind still in whichever object of beauty delights it or wherever it revels through the five senses of perception and five powers of action. A yogi should become aware, "I alone exist. I am of the form of Shiva, who is Consciousness and bliss. Everything is my own glory." In this way, he absorbs desire and other sources of agitation into himself.

By making the intellect one-pointed and still, a yogi should feel, "My own nature pulsates everywhere." Even when the mind of an ordinary person focuses on any object, whether good or bad, he forgets everything else. A yogi should increase his mental one-pointedness and become centered in that state where he, too, forgets everything else. At that point, he becomes established in his own true, blissful nature. Then his various fantasies become *nirvikalpa*, and everything is filled with Shiva. Although you are already Shiva, become Shiva. Then your heart will be filled with ecstasy.

19

Advaita Bhāva: The Attitude of Nonduality

318. A particular group of sages supporting the concept of duality asserts that although an individual performs actions, the fruits are granted according to the judgment of God. To support this view, they quote the following statement from the Upanishads: *Karmādhyaksha sarva bhūtādhivāsah sākshī chetā kevalo nirgunashcha*[59] — "God, who presides over all actions, is the attributeless Witness." The philosophies of Nyāya, Vaisheshika, Yoga, and so on, belong to this category.[60] These philosophies, which strengthen the notion of duality, have made God solely and totally transcendental. However, there is only one Supreme Principle, and it pervades the entire universe. *Ekam sat viprā bahudhā vadanti* — "Reality is one, but the wise men of different philosophies describe it in many different ways." Some call it Rām; others call it Krishna, Allāh, Parameshwara, or the Void. They call the same One by different names, but the Truth is the same for all.

Once a saint told his disciples the following story: One day four people, a Persian, an Arab, a Turk, and a Greek, went

---

59. *Shvetāshvatara Upanishad*, 6-11.

60. Three of the six main philosophies in the Indian system.

on a journey together. They had been given two rupees to spend. The Persian said, "I'll buy *angūr* with this money, and we can all eat them." The Arab said, "No, I want to buy *ināb*." The Turk said, "No, I like *üzum*. I want to buy that." The Greek said, "I don't want to buy anything but *stafyllia*." Each of them kept repeating what he wanted, without understanding the other three. Finally, they began to quarrel. *Vāde vāde vairavahni vardhate* — "The fire of enmity grows through arguments and counterarguments." They began to exchange blows. At that point, a wise man approached them and asked why they were fighting. After listening to them, he said, "Don't fight. I'll satisfy all of you. I'll bring what each of you wants." He took the money, went to a shop, and bought grapes. Then he distributed them equally among the four. The Persian said, "These are my *angūr*!" The Arab said, "Here are my *ināb*!" The Turk said, "These are my *üzum*!" And the Greek said, "Here are my *stafyllia*!" The saint who related this story told his disciples that we all need such a wise man. Even today, people who lack the eye of knowledge fight because they have blind faith in one particular doctrine. However, there is only one Supreme Principle for all, one goal, one purpose, one love.

319. Another group of sages states that Paramashiva, through His independent power, has become the material universe, which is full of various forms, modifications, and change. They state that He has also become the innumerable individual souls, who are nothing but Consciousness. The tradition of Advaita, or nonduality, accepts this theory.

320. *Advaita* means one without a second. There are many different schools of philosophy. The Mādhyamikas are Shūnyāvādins. The Yogāchāras are Vijnānavādins. The Vivartavādins are Nirvisheshādvaitins. The Shakti-

Vishishtādvaitins and Vishishtādvaitins are Savisheshād-vaitins. The Yādava Prakāshāchāryas are Brahmādvaitins. The exponents of Kashmir Shaivism are Bhedābheda Advaitins.

The word *advaita* is common to all these philosophies. All the Advaitavadins consider the world, virtue and sin, bondage and liberation to be real in one way or another. They all share one main belief — the operation of the law of *karma*. They believe that the current of *karma* has been flowing in this world of reality since the beginning of time but that it finally ends in liberation. Among these schools of Advaita, the tradition of Kashmir Shaivism belongs to the group which says that the world is not different from the Absolute. Actually it teaches that the world is both different and not different from Him, because the world is the effect of the Shakti of that Supreme Principle.

In this philosophy, the nature of *karma* is described in a unique way. Paramashiva, together with His own insepa-rable Shakti, who contains the five powers, has become both transcendental and immanent. In His transcendental state, He is completely serene, without modification, movement, or vibration. In His immanent state, He is the *grāhakas*, individual souls; *grāhya*, the world; and *grahana*, the body and the senses. For many reasons, these three appear to be different and to have different natures. In the form of indi-vidual souls, Shiva performs good or bad actions and then experiences them as pain or pleasure. In Shaivism, this is called the *karma mala*.

321. The play of creation in which unity is paramount is called *shuddha adhvā*, or the pure creation. The creation in which duality is paramount and which is characterized by multiplic-ity is called *ashuddha adhvā*, or the impure creation. As the *jnāna, icchā,* and *kriyā shaktis* become contracted one by one,

they become the *ānava*, *māyīya*, and *kārma malas*. In the pure creation there are five *tattvas*, and in the impure creation there are thirty-one *tattvas*. This makes a total of thirty-six *tattvas*. All thirty-one *tattvas* of the impure creation came into existence because of the *malas*. Without the *ānava mala*, the *māyīya mala* does not appear. The individual, whose body and senses are composed of the thirty-one principles of the *māyīya mala*, has limited knowledge and power and, due to the *kārma mala*, performs good or bad actions.

Although *jnāna*, *icchā*, and *kriyā shaktis* are closely connected to one another, *kriyā shakti* predominates in action. Actually these three things exist in all actions: to know, to desire, and to strive. If we do not know something, we have no desire for it. If we have no desire for it, we do not perform the action of striving to obtain it. This shows that there is a close connection among these *shaktis*. From the highest viewpoint, these *shaktis* are not different from one another because they belong to the one Consciousness.

322. Many actions are performed by the physical body, the subtle senses, and the subtle body, which interconnects them. These actions can either bring about one's downfall or, when they cause the expansion of knowledge, improve one's welfare. However, actions are not the true cause of the expansion of knowledge. They can only make one worthy of it.

The subject of how long one has to perform actions and when they cease is very profound. People give their own meaning to the word *karma*. According to Kashmir Shaivism, the true experience of the play of Consciousness consists of performing actions with the understanding that it is the *kriyā shakti* acting, not the individual. If a person performs actions with this understanding, they do not bind him. Knowledge, meditation, mantra repetition, and worship all help him to attain the Self. But if a person fails to understand the concept of nondoership and performs actions with ego and attachment, they bind him. This is the conviction of Shaivism.

323. One should perform actions considering them to be service to God. At the same time, one should renounce their fruits knowing that to perform actions with a sense of detachment is the natural state of *prakriti*, or nature. Through the *ānava mala*, Consciousness becomes contracted. Through the *māyīya mala*, one becomes aware of differences. Through the *kārma mala*, one performs good and bad actions. One who understands the mystery behind these things realizes that Shiva, through His play, is performing all the activities of the universe. With this understanding, a person pursues the miracle of seeing duality in unity and unity in duality. He finally attains the all-pervasive unity-awareness. He realizes *Pūrno'ham*, the perfect "I"-consciousness. As long as a person lacks the understanding of the universe and his own true nature, as long as he fails to experience the multiplicity of the universe as the play of the *shakti chakra*, the group of powers, he is bound by *karma*. However, after the awakening of the knowledge of the Truth, a person's *karmas* help to expand his knowledge.

Everyone knows the actions performed by the body and experiences the feelings and thoughts of the mind. Enlightened beings fully experience the serene state, which is devoid of both bodily and mental activities, as their true nature. This serene Consciousness is the basis of all bodily and mental activities. One should experience this through contemplation. This is called the knowledge of one's own Self. A great being is one who has turned within and who knows his own Self. What is true knowledge? It is the knowledge of the Self.

324.   The specialty of Shaivism is the complete attainment of the experience "I am Shiva." In the initial stages, a person with this cosmic awareness sees Paramashiva in everything. In the stage of mature awareness, he recognizes that he is one with Shiva. The scriptures describe the relationship between the world and the seeker in many ways. They also describe many spiritual practices which enable one to experience unity with Shiva. These are nothing more than different ways of relating to the world according to one's capacity. Although there is only one nondual Principle to be understood in Shaivism, that Principle has become dual within unity. How did this happen? One's doubts can be removed by such books as the *Shiva Drishti*, *Ishwara Pratyabhijnā*, and *Spanda Kārikā*.

The *Shiva Sūtras* are the foundation of Kashmir Shaivism. They were discovered by the great Siddha Vasugupta. To disseminate the *Shiva Sūtras*, he wrote the *Spanda Kārikā* and other books in which he explained the hidden meanings of the *sūtras*.[61] Somānanda wrote the *Shiva Drishti* and proved through logical deduction (*yukti*) and reasoning (*pramāna*) that the world and Shiva are one. After him, Utpalāchārya explained the meaning of this in a number of verses, which together became known as the *Ishwara Pratyabhijnā*. His followers, Abhinavagupta and Kshemarāja, also substantiated the doctrine of Shaivism.

Through the *Shiva Drishti*, *Ishwara Pratyabhijnā*, *Spandavivarana*, and other texts, we can obtain complete understanding and perceive, as directly as we perceive our own face in a mirror, that everything is Shiva, that our own true nature is the all-pervasive Shiva, and that the Self is Consciousness. Whether or not one reads these philosophies,

---

61. There is some controversy regarding the authorship of *Spanda Kārikā*. Although Vasugupta is generally considered the author, some claim that it was written by his great disciple Kallata.

Muktānanda says that their essence is very simple. A pot which is made of clay is still fundamentally clay. Ornaments made of gold remain gold inside and out. Cotton cloth which consists of warp and woof is still cotton. Tweezers, scissors, and knives made of steel remain steel. A son has his father's form. A daughter has her mother's form. A mango comes from a mango, a coconut from a coconut. In the same way, Shiva is the original, material, and instrumental cause of the entire universe.

The world is in Shiva, and Shiva is in the world. A coconut tree, with its extraordinary shape, springs from one coconut. Similarly, the universe, which is wondrous and full of infinite forms, springs from Shiva and exists in Shiva. The universe is Shiva, the Supreme Consciousness. Shiva pervades all forms. He exists as conscious beings and as matter. Although He is many, He is one. He is a man and a woman. He is food. He is the experiencer as well as that which is experienced. He is *nityānanda*, eternal bliss, and *ātmānanda*, the bliss of the Self. He is you and I. This is the Advaita doctrine of Shaivism.

Iti vā yasya samvittih krīdātvenākhilam jagat.[62]

The entire world is the play of Universal Consciousness. It has become the universe.

---

62. Vasugupta, *Spanda Kārikā*, II-5.

20

Shiva Drishti:
The Outlook of Shiva

325.   Everyone knows that there are two types of objects in the
universe — sentient and insentient. The universe appears
to be full of differences because it includes both matter and
conscious beings. There are definite and important reasons
for considering the universe to be Shiva, and it is essential to
know what they are. As time passes, objections to this way of
thinking will naturally arise; wherever there is a lack of
understanding, objections always arise. Shrī Somānanda,
refuting the objections which prevailed in his time, explained in one of his most sublime works, the *Shiva Drishti*,
how the universe is one with Shiva. He revealed that Shiva
is everywhere. We should wear the glasses of that same
drishti, or outlook, and see things in that way.

326.   No matter what we think, our experience is always limited
by time, space, and circumstances. Before we can understand that the universe is the embodiment of Shiva, we must
first understand these three limitations; the *Shiva Drishti*
explains in detail why and how the supremely independent
Shiva, who is never bound by these three things, accepted
such limitations. This subject will be dealt with in Chapters
22 and 23.

126

327. Paramashiva is the embodiment of Consciousness. He pulsates in all objects as Consciousness. Without being bound by anything, He expands through the *icchā* and *kriyā* *shaktis*.

> *Ātmaiva sarva bhāveshu sphuran nirvrita chidvibhuhu,*
> *Aniruddhecchā prasaraha prasarad drikkriyaha shivaha.* [63]

> Shiva Himself expands unobstructedly in all feelings through the *icchā* and *kriyā shaktis*. To regard all objects as the embodiment of Shiva is the *Shiva drishti*, the outlook of Shiva.

328. Shiva is perfect, complete, and omnipotent. He pervades equally all forms as well as formlessness. The universe is not different from Shiva. One who has this understanding sees Shiva's form everywhere. Therefore, Shankarāchārya said, *Aham brahmāsmi* — "I am the Absolute."

> *Na shivaha shakti rahito na shaktir vyatirekinī,*
> *Shivaha shaktastathā bhāvān icchayā kartumīhate.* [64]

> Shiva and Shakti are not different from each other. Because Shiva possesses Shakti, He controls the activities of this multifaceted universe.

> *Sa chitvam samsthitam nityam kathanīyam tathāgrataha,*
> *Evam sarvapadārthānām samaiva shivatā sthitā.* [65]

> *Jnāna, icchā,* and *kriyā* exist in objects which have a form and also in formless feelings. Thus, Shivahood exists in all objects.

> *Tasmāt samagrākāreshu sarvāsu pratipattishu,*
> *Vijneyam shiva rūpatvam sva shaktyā vesha nātmakam.* [66]

---

63. Somānanda, *Shiva Drishti*, I-2.
64. Ibid., III-3.
65. Ibid., I-47, 48.
66. Ibid., III-17.

Although Shiva, when moved by Shakti, exists in all perceptions, all forms, and all objects, He is still perfect. He never loses His perfection.

Evam bhedatmakam nityam shivatattvamanantakam,
Tathā tasya vyavasthānān nānārūpe'pi satyatā. [67]

Although the universe is manifold because of the constant arrangement of infinite varieties of forms, in reality only the state of Shiva exists.

Sthitam shivatvam sarvatra visheshācchaiva vādinām,
Ekatvena tato jneyā shivatā sarva gocharā. [68]

It has been proved that the state of Shiva is everywhere, in duality as well as in unity, because Shiva possesses infinite powers. A devotional person sees Shiva's form everywhere.

329. A seeker who is truly ripe does not need any *upāyas* to recognize that he is Shiva. Just as he can naturally recognize his parents, in the same way, he can recognize that he is Shiva through inference, scriptural truths, or a word from the Guru. He does not need to perform any spiritual practices. For him, the means of attainment (*upāya*) and the goal which is attained (*upeya*), the attainment (*prāpya*) and the one who attains (*prāpaka*), the enjoyer (*bhoktā*) and that which is enjoyed (*bhogya*) are all forms of Shiva.

Ekavāram pramānena shāstrādvā guruvākyataha,
Jnāte shivatve sarvasthe pratipatyā dridhātmanā. [69]

One who has firm conviction easily attains the experience of perfection in his own state by knowing Shiva. This comes through scriptural inference or just one word from the Guru.

---

67. Ibid., I-29.
68. Ibid., IV-126, 127.
69. Ibid., VII-5, 6.

Shivo'smi sādhanā vishtaha shivo'ham yājako'pyaham.
Shivam yāmi shivo yāmi shivena shiva sādhanaha. [70]

Practice *sādhanā* with the following awareness: "I am
a form of Shiva. I will attain Shiva. By becoming
Him, I will attain Him. Because I am Shiva, I will
attain Shivahood very easily." This is the *sādhanā* to
attain Shiva.

Bhinno'pyabhinna evāsmi shiva ittham vicheshtanam,
Shivo bhoktā shivo bhojyam shiveshu shiva sādhanaha. [71]

Although I appear to be different, I am one with
Shiva. The entire universe is the activity of Shiva.
Shiva experiences everything. It is essential to know
Shiva. Being Shiva, I will attain Him. Shiva is the
experiencer as well as what is experienced. While
remaining Shiva, I will attain Him.

Shivaha kartā shivaha karma shivo'smi karanātmakaha. [72]

Shiva is the doer of everything. He is also the action.
Although I am involved with all my senses, I am still
Shiva.

In this way, by becoming established in the awareness of
Shiva, by knowing Shiva, a mature seeker becomes one with
Him. This is the essence of the *Shiva drishti*. In the *Yoga
Vāsishtha*, it is said, *Yā drishtihi sā srishtihi* — "The world is as
you see it."

330. The blissful Paramashiva both transcends the universe and
is the universe. He is the highest bliss and nothing but a mass
of light. He makes the entire universe from Shiva to the
earth come into existence, yet always remain one with

---

70. Ibid., VII-96, 98.
71. Ibid., VII-99.
72. Ibid., VII-100.

Himself. Actually, in that state, there is no other subject or object. The supreme, blissful Shiva alone manifests Himself in the innumerable forms of multiplicity.

331. The creation experienced by one ignorant person differs from that of another. A person's creation depends on his understanding. However, for one who knows the Truth, the entire world is the embodiment of Shiva.

> *Aham shivaha shivaschāyam tvam chāpi shiva eva hi,*
> *Sarvam shivamayam brahma shivāt param na kinchana.*

> I am Shiva and Shiva is me. You are also Shiva. Everything is Shiva. Everything is Brahman. Everything is Consciousness. There is nothing different from Shiva.

Neha nānāsti kinchana — "There is no multiplicity here whatsoever." There is nothing which is different from Shiva. This is *Shiva drishti*, the outlook of Shiva. This is the outlook of the Self. This is the outlook of spirituality. Any outlook other than this is blindness.

21

Pravrittivāda:
The Theory of Extroversion

332. The contraction of Shakti is the fundamental cause of the
      state of individuality. In this contracted state, a person
      always focuses outside himself. He is always extroverted, and
      so limitless desires torture him in every possible way. If he is
      alone, he wants to become two; he wants a mate. If he is
      married, he wants a house. Then he wants to have children
      or to expand his business. Desire can never know content-
      ment. Just as darkness cannot comprehend the sun, a desire
      can never experience satisfaction or fulfillment. In the king-
      dom of desires, satisfaction and contentment have never
      taken birth.

      Desires are always increasing. The more we encourage
      them, the more they flourish. They can never be satisfied.
      Even if our desires obtained all three worlds, they would still
      keep growing. No matter how many means we use to placate
      them, they continue to swell. If we satisfy the body, our
      mental desires multiply. There is no way to fulfill desires
      through limited objects. Anxiety, fear, doubts, and the
      innumerable offspring of jealousy continue to proliferate in
      the wake of desire. The progeny of extroversion overrun the
      world. Only when extroversion merges into the infinite

Supreme Principle are all its desires fulfilled. Only then do they cease to exist. The attainment of this state of universality is called *moksha*, or liberation.

Even after dwelling on limited things for a long time, one does not attain peace. This is why the belief has arisen that it is better to reject them. Believing this with great intensity, some scholars renounce mundane activities and the outer world. They explain that the world should be renounced because it is imaginary, illusory, and full of momentary pain and pleasure. The truth is that no matter what lectures a person may give, no matter what books or dramas he may write from birth to death, he cannot become free of these imaginary but naturally created limitations and the pain and pleasure which arise from them.

333.   A person can lead a joyful life in the world and experience universal brotherhood if he has the inner knowledge that the external world is the embodiment of God. He should also have the firm conviction that the people of the world are all God, and perform virtuous actions with peace, with good feelings, and without deception or expectations. If he leads his life in the world without expectations, he will attain happiness and contentment.

22

The Cause of Bondage

334   As long as the individual soul is affected by *māyā shakti*[73] and considers the universe to be different from himself, he will remain bound. In reality, this world, which is the play of Shakti, is his own body. Considering the world to be other than himself is the cause of his bondage. Attachment and aversion, enmity and jealousy, and other kinds of misery arise from the idea that the knower and the known are separate. The individual soul performs good or bad actions through the influence of these sources of misery. Impressions of old desires and the fruits of actions ultimately ripen and give birth to infinite impurities. If a person recognizes his own true nature through the power of pure knowledge, he becomes free. Through pure knowledge, bondage dissolves.

> *Eshah pramātā māyāndhaha samsāri karma bandhanaha,*
> *Vidyā bhijñāpi taishvaryaha chidghano mukta uchyate.* [74]

> The individual soul, through the power of *māyā*, falls into the bondage of *karma* and is subject to the law of transmigration. Through true knowledge, he is made to recognize his power and then, because he is pure Consciousness, he is called liberated.

---

73. The power which creates differentiation.
74. Utpalāchārya, *Īshwara Pratyabhijñā*, III-2-2.

23

Release from Bondage

335. Three impurities, or *malas* —*ānava mala, māyīya mala*, and *kārma mala* —exist in everyone, from gods to human beings.

Apurnoham manyatārūpam ānava malam — "*Ānava mala* is the notion 'I am imperfect.'" Although the individual soul is perfect, he considers himself imperfect. This is the *ānava mala*, which comes into being because of the contraction of *icchā shakti*, the power of will. The *ānava mala* causes the omnipresent Paramashiva to lose His all-pervasiveness and become a limited individual. *Anātmanyātmābhimānam* — "To identify oneself with the non-Self, the body, and so on, is the *ānava mala.*"

The *māyīya mala* also comes into existence because of a contraction of *icchā shakti*. *Bhinnavedya prathā* — "It brings about a sense of difference." Even though Chiti is nondual and all-pervasive, through the *māyīya mala* it experiences duality. The body is enveloped by the *pancha kanchukas*, or five limitations of Shakti, and is under the control of the senses. This is the effect of the *māyīya mala*.

The *kārma mala* is the cause of *shubha ashubha anushtā-nam* — good and bad actions — performed through the senses of perception, the powers of action, and the mind.

Birth is caused by actions. From good actions, one reaps good fruit. From bad actions, one reaps bad fruit. The *karma mala* follows an individual through countless births in the form of impressions and tendencies.

A limited individual's experience consists of the three states of waking, dream, and deep sleep. His world is made of these states and the *malas*. While the individual is in bondage, he identifies with the void of the deep sleep state, the *prāna*, the subtle body, and the physical body. Through the Guru, the knowledge of the scriptures, his own efforts, and the understanding that he is independent, all-pervasive, eternal, and perfect, he transcends all his ordinary experiences and feelings. The different *upāyas*, chanting hymns to God, offering salutations, repeating the mantra *Om Namah Shivāya*, worship, meditation, the practices leading to *samā-dhi*, and other spiritual activities are all taught in order to facilitate this transformation. With the help of these things, a person's knowledge expands, and he experiences the bliss of Consciousness. As long as his body is alive, he lives happily. Once his body dies, he becomes one with Paramashiva.

24

Samvit Parāmarsha: The Comprehension of the Supreme "I"-Consciousness

336. On one hand, our experience leads us to believe that matter and consciousness are inseparable. On the other hand, we experience matter as inert objects, different from consciousness. We know that ultimately the experience of matter as separate — as *idam*, "this" — evolves into *samvit parāmarsha*, the experience of the supreme "I"-consciousness. For this reason, we think that only conscious entities have the power of consciousness and that inert objects lack it. Both of these experiences are the play of God, who assumes the form of the universe.

> *Svātmaiva sarvajantūnām eka eva maheshwaraha,*
> *Vishva rūpo'ha midamit yakhandā marsha branhitaha.*
>
> Only the Self, God, who has taken the form of the universe, exists in all beings. By ceaselessly contemplating "I am He," a person blissfully experiences the entire universe as his own Self.

Through its independent power, the infinite "I"-consciousness plays in the form of both "I" and "this." In the experience of perfect "I"-consciousness, there is no distinction of place or time. If this differentiation arises, Consciousness takes the form of the world of objects. This is where the difference arises between the two experiences mentioned above. By contracting His power, God creates the world, or *idam*. He assumes many forms: the intellect, *prāna*, the physical body, and so on. Limited by duality, the partial "I"-consciousness experiences, "I am different." In this way, because we lack the knowledge of our own true nature, we have become rooted in duality, in the idea that we are many. Therefore, such concepts as "I am the experiencer," "This is joyful," and "That is painful" have multiplied.

Sva svarūpa parijñāna mayo'nekaha pumān mataha,
Tatra srishtau kriya nando bhogo dukha sukhat makaha.

A person creates pain and pleasure and becomes troubled by forgetting his own Self and getting caught up in the knowledge of duality, by limiting his own perfection and accepting imperfection, and by creating duality with the understanding "I am different from others."

337. When a person acquires the knowledge of his own true nature, the pure "I"-awareness, his old world changes into a new one filled with joy, bliss, love, and God. The entire world is the play of the Universal Consciousness.

25

Shiva Samāvesha:
Union with Shiva

338.   In God, the *jnāna*, *icchā*, and *kriyā shaktis* remain pure. In a
bound soul, they are impure because of *māyā*. In this state, in
which one considers the separate objects of the world to be
devoid of awareness, there arise the three *gunas* — *sattva*
(purity), *rajas* (activity), and *tamas* (inertia). *Sattva* is characterized by pleasure (*prakāsha*), and its function is knowledge. *Rajas* is characterized by pain (*aprakāsha*), and its
function is action (*kriyā*). *Tamas* is characterized by the
deluded state in which one experiences neither pleasure nor
pain (*avaprakāsha*), and its function is restriction (*niyamana*). The soul, therefore, experiences joy through purity,
pain through activity, and illusion or wrong understanding
through inertia. Through the influence of the *gunas*, different kinds of understanding arise within. They are all reflections of the power of the Supreme Consciousness. The mental
creation of the bound soul is of two types: one is imagination of
what is actual, such as visualizing the warp and woof of cloth,
and the other is deluded imagination, such as believing a
rope to be a snake. Both are creations of the mind. When
these thoughts disappear through the awareness of *Shivo'-
ham* — "I am Shiva" — a person acquires the certainty that

138

the entire universe is one with God. As this knowledge becomes firmly rooted in him, he becomes a *jivanmukta* (a being who is liberated while still in the body), even though isolated thoughts continue to arise within him.

Sarvo mamāyam vibhava ityevam parijānataha,
Vishvātmano vikalpānām prasare'pi maheshatā. [75]

He who has realized his identity with the universe, and who knows that all that is manifest is simply his glory, possesses the status of the highest Lord, even when thoughts and images are still arising in him.

Such a liberated soul becomes established in the awareness of Shiva and considers all the thoughts which arise and subside in the space of Consciousness to be like clouds coming and going in the sky.

339. This is the difference between a bound soul and an enlightened being. A yogi who has attained true knowledge considers all the principles from Shiva through Sadāshiva down to insects as one. To him everything is *aham*, or "I." *Samatā sarvabhūtānām samata sarvavallīnām* — "He sees equality in all beings, trees, and creepers." For him, the entire world is *prameya*, that which is known, and he remains one with it. He also considers himself one with the knowers, or *prāmātris*. However, the understanding of a bound soul is different from this. A bound soul considers the knower to be different from that which is known.

Joy and pain, enmity and friendship, bondage and liberation, and supreme bliss all arise within and are simply a matter of understanding. Maintaining the right understanding is one's *sādhanā* as well as its fruit. An individual who

---

75. Abhinavagupta, *Īshwara Pratyabhijñā Vimarshinī*, IV-1-12.

considers himself to be God, and who considers his powers of knowledge and action to be manifestations of God's independent freedom, experiences God's cosmic form. Such a seeker merges into God and becomes Him when his body dies.

The *Bhagavad Gītā* says, *Bahirantascha bhūtānām acharam charameva cha*[76] — "He dwells equally in all sentient beings and insentient objects." Although fire appears in different forms, its heat is the same in all of them. In the same way, God pervades all objects and beings subtly and eternally. He is one, within and without, near and far, everywhere. His nature never changes. He is Shiva.

---

76. *Bhagavad Gītā*, XIII-15.

26

Jnāna Svarūpa: The True Nature of Knowledge

340. It is natural for the question to arise, "When we see an object, where do we get our understanding of that object?" Knowledge does not come only from external objects. In fact, some people know nothing about a particular object even though they come in contact with it. Others may be indifferent to that object. There are also people on whom an object makes no impression even though they make an effort to perceive it. Therefore, we cannot say that external objects necessarily give rise to knowledge. Of course, external objects are necessary to create either joy or agitation through our outer senses. But the knowledge which we derive from such words as heaven, hell, Kailāsa, and Vaikuntha does not depend on the physical existence of these places. Such knowledge springs from a definite center in the realm of our feelings. It does not need the same kind of basis as the knowledge which arises from contact with external objects.

For example, our lives are primarily focused on the belief in virtue and sin. This tendency, which makes us think that bad actions are wrong and good actions are right, does not need any outer support. The tendency can be understood by its own reality, which is also its motivating force. For a person who has faith and who understands the state of Shiva, that understanding is not different from its impulse, which is *kriyā shakti*. In other words, all these kinds of understanding are not different from the Supreme Principle.

341. Yogis do not view their understanding as different from the Supreme Principle, their true inner nature. The inner Principle with its own vibration arises as one's limited understanding. This understanding gives an object definite characteristics — for example, "This is a mango; it is red, round, and weighs two kilos." Even though the experience of these characteristics is limited, still it is the result of the vibration of Consciousness as *jnāna shakti*, the power of knowledge.

Since *jnāna shakti* is a vibration of Consciousness, the result of its play is also not different from Consciousness. In other words, when the vibration becomes limited, objects are perceived with limited vision. This understanding is called *grāhya grāhaka bhāva* — awareness of the subject-object relationship. When a person says, "I see this object," that "I" is the *grāhaka bhāva* — the awareness of the perceiver. "This object" is the *grāhya bhāva* — the awareness of the perceived. The awareness of both the perceiver and the perceived vibrates in the *pramātri*, or knower. These differences, however, are all vibrations of the Truth. "This is a mountain," "This is a piece of fruit," "This is a man" — all of these constant vibrations of the perceived actually are not different from the perceiver.

In reality, everything is the vibration of the Supreme Principle. The perceiver and the perceived are both forms of the same Principle. If a person gives up his ego through right understanding, he naturally uplifts himself and becomes the true Absolute. Otherwise, like a silkworm enclosed in a cocoon, he becomes trapped in the beauty of his own body and forgets himself. Then he becomes his own enemy.

342. Therefore, a person should seek his own Self and understand the world. He should know God who permeates the forms of the world. When he understands and knows his own Self, all his old impressions subside. He never again feels, "I am different from God and God is far away from me." When filth and squalor are removed, only purity is left. Similarly, when the war of thoughts and doubts comes to an end, the individual becomes God. When a person's identification with the body is totally destroyed, he need do nothing else to become God because he has been completely saturated with God all along. His experience is "I am in God and God is in me." Moreover, he experiences the entire universe as being filled with God. This kind of understanding is *jñāna svarūpa*, the true nature of knowledge.

27

Pratibhā:
The Light of Consciousness

343. The power through which we understand what a particular
object is or through which we obtain any kind of knowledge
is called *pratibhā*. For example, we know that a certain
object is a pen. The power through which we realize that it is
a pen is called *pratibhā*. The power of *pratibhā* is one with
pramātri, the knower. We usually obtain knowledge of different objects singly and sequentially, one after another. When
we are discussing one subject, other subjects do not come up.
When we are reflecting on one object, we do not think of
other objects. But when we look at a picture with a forest, an
ocean, a tree, and a creeper painted in different colors, we do
not get a clear-cut impression of each separate object. Instead, we receive collective knowledge of the whole mass.
Later, as we notice each separate object, we forget our
previous collective knowledge of it. In this way, the consciousness of the whole exists before the understanding
which comes in sequence. That nondual and nonsequential
consciousness, *pratibhā*, is the Knower: God.

Yā chaishā pratibhā tat tat padārtha krama rūshitā,
Akramā nanta chidrūpaha pramātā sa maheshwaraha. [77]

That consciousness which is colored by or identified
with the succession of different objects is nothing
other than the great Lord, the highest Knower, and
nothing but the unchanging light of Consciousness.

344. *Pratibhā* is the force behind inner inspiration. It is a wondrous light and an extraordinary experience. It is God's
power, the light of the Self. It exists in God eternally. The
moment this Shakti unfolds, the entire world expands.

345. One can attain *pratibhā* by destroying thoughts and past
impressions and through *shaktipāt*, or the grace of Shiva. A
being who has attained *pratibhā* eliminates all thoughts and
experiences and so can remove the obstacles which prevent
him from seeing his own true nature. He can directly know
the past, present, and future. He can have a vision of the
incredible Pārameshwarī, the Supreme Shakti. He can fash-
ion a new creation within himself because *pratibhā* gives
rise to ever-new creative abilities.

The One who controls the activities of the mundane world
with its different varieties of knowledge is called the Knower.
This Knower determines cause and effect by combining the
past and that which we have already seen with the present
and that which we see now, and so on. Thus, we acquire our
knowledge of that which exists and that which does not
exist, of obstructions and that which is being obstructed. New
thoughts and feelings continually arise along with the power
to discriminate between an object and its *dharma*, or inherent
nature. In this way, in the principle of *pratibhā*, both pure and

---

77. Utpalāchārya, *Īshwara Pratyabhijnā*, I-7-7.

impure activities occur. This principle is composed of various
kinds of understanding which are mutually opposed.

346. The understandings which arise in us are momentary.
They are all relative and merely *ābhāsas*, or reflections.
Although we have different thoughts, which consist of variations of the past, present, and future, only one Being is the
substratum of them all. We can divide our experiences into
four categories: joyful, painful, those which cause joy, and
those which cause pain. We think that wealth brings joy and
that violence, poverty, and so on, bring pain. When we
come in contact with objects, pain and pleasure arise. We
experience joy when we obtain the objects that we desire; as
long as we do not have them, we are not happy. In addition,
we have the mistaken idea that all the efforts which we put
forth to attain happiness are also joyful. Once we have
enjoyed the desired object, all that remains is the reflection
of thoughts, the memory; through delusion, we also consider
that to be joy.

Actually happiness is the reflection of the vibration of
jñāna shakti, the power of knowledge. It is not tied to objects.
Although a renunciant and a greedy person have the same
right to wealth, the renunciant, because he understands
these *ābhāsas*, values renunciation whereas the greedy person
gives more importance to indulging in pleasure. The more
we think about pain or pleasure, the more we conclude that
they are merely *ābhāsas*.

> *Sukhādishu cha saukhyādi hetushvapi cha vastushu,*
> *Avabhāsasya sadbhāve'p yatītatvāt tathā sthitihi.* [78]

> Although *ābhāsas* such as pleasure, or those which
> are the means thereof, remain always the same, they
> manifest differently because they are unified with
> another *ābhāsa*, namely, "past."

---

78. Utpalāchārya, *Īshwara Pratyabhijnā*, I-8-3.

347. There are differences among external objects. Moreover, these objects arise, come, and go. At one moment they exist and then they do not. Therefore, they do not have absolute existence. Because the inner Principle is of the nature of absolute existence, there are differences only in its vibrations, not in that Principle itself. The reflections of Consciousness manifest outwardly as thoughts. The willpower, or *icchā shakti*, of the inner Knower brings about the experiences of pain and pleasure which arise from external objects. In this way, as the Shakti of the Knower flows outward, inner and outer activities go on through the powers of knowledge and action. All understanding, both inner and outer, is considered to be due to the power of *pratibhā* awareness. Good company, discussion of the Truth, the gift of *shaktipāt*, and God's grace are paramount in bringing about the direct knowledge of *pratibhā*.

28

Avabhāsa and Ābhāsādrishti: Seeing the World as a Reflection

348. The knowledge of the objects which can be perceived at any moment is first found within the knower. These objects are then seen outside. For this reason, they are called *ābhāsas* (or *avabhāsas*), reflections. The main characteristic of these reflections is *asānkarya*, which denotes the fact that they do not merge together and refers to inner understandings and outer objects which are mutually opposed or different from one another. These are like fire and camphor which are reflected in the same mirror but do not interact. (The opposite of this is *sānkarya*, a blend. Two things have to mix in order to become *sānkarya*.) In this way, the objects that we experience appear to be different from one another. However, the reflection and the reflected object are one and the same. Even though the manifested objects may remain separate from one another, they are not different from the reflecting subject. So, essentially, all the objects of experience are one. The knowledge of objects which arises in us is neither a product of our imagination nor an experience of past impressions.

349. The experiencing subject in the form of pure Consciousness unceasingly manifests the universe of infinite forms

which exists within it, even though there is no tangible material for such a manifestation. This is the play of its *icchā shakti*, or willpower. There are testimonies and stories of how yogis and Siddhas who had achieved oneness with Consciousness created entire universes merely through their willpower. In the same way, only objects which exist within can be reflected outside.

> *Vartamānā vabhāsānām bhāvānā mavabhāsanam,*
> *Antasthitāvatameva ghatate bahirātmanā.*[79]

> The inner Self continually manifests outwardly the objects which exist in its inner consciousness through its thought.

350. *Vimarsha* is the subject's act of examination of its own inner thoughts or feelings.

> *Vimarsho hi sarvam saha paramapi ātmīkaroti,*
> *Ātmanam cha paṅkaroti ubhayam ekīkaroti,*
> *Ekākrutam dvayamapi nyagbhāvyati ityevam svabhāvaha.*

> *Vimarsha* is everything. It makes itself others and makes others itself. It can make one into two, make two into one, or make everything disappear. That is its nature.

Vimarsha is the action of Chiti. It marks the difference between insentient objects and conscious beings. An inert rock does not examine itself and say, "I am." This means that it lacks knowledge of Consciousness; it is insentient because it cannot attain the awareness "I am unlimited Consciousness." Experiencing subjects, as opposed to insentient objects, are aware of their existence as "I" and have the potential of knowing themselves as Consciousness. Ordinarily they ex-

---

79. Abhinavagupta, *Ishwara Pratyabhijñā Vimarshinī*, I-5-13.

perience insentient objects as *idam*, "this." The play of this *vimarsha shakti* is infinite. *Vimarsha shakti*, by manifesting differences between subject and object, creates desire.

In this state of inner examination, whatever we have accumulated within has not yet manifested as letters and words but remains in undifferentiated seed form. These seeds are the cause of the various activities created by letters. These letters are symbolic expressions of *māyā*. Freedom is the essential nature of the source from which these letters arise. It does not depend on anything. This is discussed at length in the Shaivite literature.

351. When I say, "I see this object," it is a manifestation of *jñāna shakti,* or the power of knowledge. This manifestation is called *spanda. Spanda* is the throb or movement of God. When there is even the slightest movement of Consciousness, the knowledge of manifold objects arises.

352. *Vimarsha shakti* manifests externally in the form of *māyā shakti*, the power of illusion. At that time, it makes us aware of duality, and we experience differences through such words as knowledge, determination, and perseverance. When we analyze our understanding in a subtle way, two things become clear: first, the understanding which is connected with name and form, and second, the understanding of pure being, which transcends the limitations of name and form. This pure being is called *sat*. The word *sat* cannot be ascribed a definite meaning. Generally, when we say *sat*, we mean "that which exists forever." It exists as an eternal principle, even in all objects. However, it is very difficult to prove this because something which has no name or form cannot be grasped through empirical knowledge.

The truth is that the principle of *sat* exists even in empirical knowledge. It can also be perceived in objects. The

ancient seers said that objects have the following five aspects: *asti*, existence; *bhāti*, the act of shining; *priya*, joy;
nāma, name; and *rūpa*, form. *Priya*, *nāma*, and *rūpa* belong
to the category of that which is experienced. *Asti* and *bhāti*
are associated with the Supreme Principle. Although the
Reality which is known as pure existence cannot be limited
by time and space, it is still one with them. That Principle of
pure existence in itself does not appear with name and form
as *idam*, "this." In its immanent aspect, it appears as *idam*
through the powers of knowledge, memory, and reasoning,
but still, in its transcendental aspect, it is different from
them.

> *Ghato'yamit yadhyavasānām rūpāti rekini,*
> *Paresh shakti rātmeva bhāsate na tvidantayā.* [80]

The Shakti of Shiva shines as the Self by transcending such perceptions of name and form as "This is a
pot."

From this, we conclude that all the innumerable *ābhāsas* are
merely the play of that Chitshakti, or Consciousness.

---

80. Utpalāchārya, *Ishwara Pratyabhijñā.*

29

Spanda Nirnaya:
The Discussion of Spanda

353. The *Shiva Sutras* are the basic treatise of Kashmir Shaivism. The Siddha Vasugupta wrote commentaries on these *sutras* and brought about a revival of interest in Kashmir Shaivism. His book, *Spanda Karika*, contains fifty-one verses explaining the main principles concealed in the *Shiva Sutras*. In this way, he disseminated them. The principles explained in these verses of the *Spanda Karika* are based on the experience of Siddhas and on the *Agama Shastras*, divinely revealed texts. The *Spanda Karika* is divided into three chapters: *Svarupa Spanda, Sahaja Vidyodaya Spanda,* and *Vibhuti Spanda.* The *Svarupa Spanda* explains the nature of the Supreme Principle and describes how limitations have concealed our true nature. The *Sahaja Vidyodaya Spanda* explains how to discriminate between that which is external and that which is not, how to remain awake to the Self at all times, and also how to attain the knowledge of one's own Self. The *Vibhuti Spanda* describes the glory of Shiva and the true awareness of Him.

30

Spanda Svarūpa: The Nature of Spanda

354. *Spandate mama chakshuhu* — "My eyelids are fluttering." *Ghatāt tailam spandate* — "Oil is glistening in a pot." The word *spanda* is commonly used in these ways. The following words are synonyms for *spanda*, or movement: *sphota*, explosion; *sphurana*, throb; *chalana*, motion; *kampana*, trembling; *udaya*, arising; *unmesha*, expansion; *ābhāsana*, reflection; *nishyanda*, flux; and *unmīlana*, unfolding. *Spanda shakti* is the true nature of Paramashiva. This pure Supreme Principle reflects the totality of the thirty-six *tattvas*. This Principle is the deity which is the basis of all knowledge. It is the vital force of all mantras. It is the glory of Consciousness which has manifested in the form of Chitshakti and which has enveloped the entire universe.

355. The ordinary meaning of *spanda* is throb or vibration. In the terminology of Shaivism, the word *spanda* has a specific meaning. It refers to movement in something which was formerly motionless. *Spanda* is Shakti, the power which transcends the senses. It is the Shakti which manifests from Shiva. The word *spanda* means subtle movement or the manifestation of the subtle and pure "I"-consciousness. We should not consider the *spanda* of the pure "I"-consciousness to be like the elements violently lashing the trees during a

storm. We should understand the nature of *spanda* as the mere readiness of the Supreme Lord, who is the totality of Consciousness, to manifest as the outer universe by His own will using His independent Shakti. The nature of His *spanda* is nothing but pure "I"-consciousness. The perfect Shiva manifests this universe through His *spanda shakti*. In its very essence, *spanda shakti* is constant vibration. *Svātman yucchalanātmakaha* — "*Spanda* is the leaping up of the Lord's own Shakti." With the same *spanda*, He also dissolves the universe.

Svashakti-prachayo'sya vishvam — "The universe is the unfolding of Shiva's power." *Spanda* is the first throb which takes place when Shakti expands. *Spanda shakti* exists in Shiva in an irregular or spontaneous form and reveals outwardly all the manifestations of the universe. The great beings define it as the five actions of Shiva: creation, sustenance, dissolution, concealment, and bestowal of grace.

356. Ordinary *spanda* is nothing but the predominant active aspect of *vimarsha shakti*, the dynamic creative power which coexists with *prakāsha*, the static aspect of Paramashiva. A period of rest occurs in *spanda* when the inner "I"-consciousness is in an undifferentiated form. It also occurs when the universe has manifested outwardly and when the universe is contemplated inwardly as *idam*. Only the universal *spanda shakti* has this freedom and infinite power.

Yasyonmesha nimeshābhyām jagatah pralayodayau,
Tam shakti chakra vibhava prabhavam shankaram stumaha.[81]

We offer our salutations to that Shiva who is the fountainhead of all glory manifest in the *shakti chakra* and at whose waking and sleeping the world is created and dissolved.

---

81. Vasugupta, *Spanda Kārikā*, I-10.

31

Spanda Lakshana:
The Definition of Spanda

357. A person cannot do his work merely because he wants to do it. The instruments of the senses cannot function simply by his willing them to do so. To do his work in the way that he wants, he needs the help of the senses, but there is another force which motivates the senses and gives them the power to work. This conscious force in its introverted aspect is called the *spanda* principle. It is also called *ātmā-bala-sparsha* — the inspiration coming from contact with the strength of the Self. Through this contact with the Supreme Principle, the senses obtain the ability to carry out their work. It is this contact with the Supreme Power which is termed *spanda shakti* in our mundane experience.

Spanda *shakti* is also the grace-bestowing power in Gurus who give *shaktipāt*. Because the touch predominates in this *shakti*, we can understand the glory of Shakti through the touch and will of such Gurus.

358. The essential nature of the *spanda shakti* is the perfect, pure "I"-consciousness in the form of an initial flash or throb. Through this throb, the same Shakti manifests in infinite forms.

Shivasyaikā mahāshaktihi shivashchaiko hyanādimān,
Sā shaktir bhidyate devi bhedai rānantya shāmbhavi. [82]

In Shiva, She manifests in infinite shapes and appears as the innumerable and unique forms of the universe.

As She vibrates eternally, She is called *spanda shakti.* That Shakti is not different from Shiva.

Na shivaha shakti rahito na shaktihi shiva varjitā,
Ubhayo rāsti tādātmyam vahni dāhakayoriva.

That *spanda shakti* is not different from Shiva, because Shiva is not different from Shakti. Both Shiva and Shakti refer to the same Reality, just as fire and heat are not two different things.

In other words, *spanda shakti* is the Sublime Reality.

Sā sphurattā māhāsattā.

This vibrating Shakti is the Supreme Reality.

Sattā cha bhāvanā kartritvā sarva kriyāsu svātantryam.

Because it is the Supreme Reality, it has the freedom to perform any action.

It gives birth to every visible object that exists in the world. In addition, through the imagination, it even brings into being objects which do not exist at all from the standpoint of direct perception: *sā cha kha pushpādikamapi vyāpnoti* — "for example, a flower in the sky." A flower in the sky, the son of a barren woman, and horns on a hare are all figments of the imagination. In addition to these, *spanda shakti* also gives birth to limitations of time, space, and form. But because it is all-pervasive, it itself is not limited. *Desha kāla visheshinī* — "Space, time, and form are separate." All the objects of the universe are forms of *spanda shakti.*

---

82. *Svacchanda Tantra,* 11-27.

32

Spanda Nirdesha:
The Indication of Spanda

359. We can recognize the principle of *spanda* through all the fluctuations that occur in us. We can recognize it in the waveless state which we experience within for a fraction of a moment when we are involved in such activities as reading, running, or being afraid, furious, or astonished and also while we are pronouncing the syllables known as *visargas*. It can be neither clearly defined nor understood by others.

> *Sā cha drishyā hriduddeshe kārya smarana kālataha,*
> *Praharshā veda samaye darasandarshana kshane.*
> *Anālochanato drishte visarga prasarāspade,*
> *Visargokti prasange cha vāchane dhāvane tatha.*
> *Eteshveva prasangeshu sarva shakti vilolatā.* [83]

This means that we experience stillness for a fraction of a moment while reading, running, being afraid, furious, astonished, and pronouncing *visargas*. We experience that stillness in the first moment of meeting someone we love and in our astonishment as we watch a magic show. We can recognize the *spanda* principle in this state which lasts a fraction of a moment.

---

83. Somānanda, *Shiva Drishti*, I-9, 10, 11.

Vichitra rachanā nānākārya srishti pravartane,
Bhavat yunmukhitā chitta secchāyāhā prathamā tutihi. [84]

When the readiness arises to create diversity outside, that is the first movement of the *icchā shakti* of
Consciousness.

That readiness is *spanda*.

360. The expansion of *spanda shakti* takes two forms — general
and specific — and therefore Shaivites have given it two
names: *sāmānya spanda*, or general *spanda*, and *visesha spanda*,
or specific *spanda*. In its general form, it is unity in diversity.
In its specific form, it is diversity in unity. The general form
of that *spanda shakti* is the immanent, subtle Consciousness
or *prāna*, which pervades all the innumerable objects of the
universe. In its specific form, duality predominates, and the
spanda shakti becomes the many unique names, forms, and
objects of experience.

The power of *spanda* is free and eternal, flowing inward and
outward simultaneously. *Spanda* is the power which throbs
unceasingly. When the world began, there was an initial
explosion or pulsation. Scientists also recognize that this
vibratory power created the world and is constantly throb-
bing in the universe. It has existed since the beginning of
time and will continue to pulsate eternally.

361. God's own initial *spanda*, or throb, has become sound and
vibrates incessantly. The world exists within us in a seed
form. It is *spanda* which manifests it outwardly on such a
colossal scale.

---

84. Ibid., I-8.

Ya sā shaktir jagaddhātuhu kathitā samavāyinī,
Icchāttvam tasya sā devī sisruksho pratipadyate.[85]

When God's independent Shakti, who is inseparable from Him, is ready to flow out into the forms of
the universe, She first takes the form of *icchā*.

The *Rig Veda* states that before the moment of creation,
the Lord said, *Eko'ham bahusyāmaha*[86] — "I am alone; let
Me become many." As that *icchā shakti* unfolds, it manifests
as *jnāna shakti* and *kriyā shakti*.

Evam saishā dvirūpāpi punarbhedairanekatām,
Arthopādhivashādyāti chintāmaniriveshwari.

Because the Shakti in Her supremacy possesses both
the power of knowledge and the power of action,
She is the wish-fulfilling gem.[87]

She continually unfolds in order to create objects (*prameya*)
and branches out in infinite currents. As a result, She expands to form the multiplicity of the universe, from Shiva to
the earth. Shakti, through the power of knowledge, flows
through the three paths of *varna*, *pada*, and *mantra*.[88]
Through the power of action, She flows through the other
three paths of *kalā*, *tattva*, and *bhuvana*.[89] In this way, She
assumes the forms of the outer universe. The expansion of
the entire universe of sound takes place in the form of the
first three paths, and the universe of matter in the form of the
latter three paths. Both of these come into existence through
spanda.

---

85. *Mālinī Vijaya Tantra*, 3-5.
86. *Rig Veda*, 1-104-46.
87. A jewel mentioned in the scriptures as having the power to fulfill all desires.
88. See Glossary.
89. See Glossary.

33

Anusandhāna of Spanda Shakti
Contemplation of Spanda Shakti

362. *Ekachintā prasaktasya yatah syādaparodayaha,*
    Unmeshaha sa tu vijneyaha svayam tam upalakshayet.[90]

    The experience which arises within us when we
    move from one thought or feeling to another is
    called *unmesha*. One should know it by looking
    within.

    This must be understood primarily through experience. From
    one vibration, another arises. *Bindu* (light), *nāda* (sound),
    rūpa (form), *rasa* (taste), and so on, arise from *spanda*.

363. Through the power of *spanda*, an ignorant person is driven to
    perform actions. Even if he has spiritual longing, because of
    the influence of *spanda* he does not notice it. When the
    experience of *aham*, "I am," arises everywhere, one can see
    the *spanda* principle governing omniscience and the other
    qualities associated with it.

364. Through effort, a person can come to know the true nature
    of the universe. But even after he knows it, he must be

---

90. Kshemarāja, *Spanda Nirnaya*, IV-2.

vigilant. Only if he seeks the Supreme Principle one-pointedly will he avoid being tortured by other things.

> *Prabhuddhah sarvadā tishthet jñānenā lochya gocharam,*
> *Ekatraropayet sarvam tato'nyena na pīdyate.* [91]

A yogi should be very alert after achieving the true vision of the world. He should maintain awareness of the unity of the whole, and then there will be no "other" to trouble him.

In other words, if, through knowledge, a person one-pointedly contemplates the *spanda* of the universe, then the world of duality causes him no trouble or pain.

365. Infinite powers arise from groups of letters. One who falls victim to them is ignorant. An ignorant person is not independent because he lacks the feeling of supreme bliss. Groups of letters are always ready to conceal his true nature. Bondage consists of not knowing the glory of the *shakti chakra* (the group of powers which control the inner and outer worlds), whereas liberation and all other attainments are the result of knowing it. A person who is bound and under the control of the mind, intellect, ego, and subtle body experiences pain and pleasure. This is called *samsāra*, or worldly existence.

> *Seyam kriyātmikā shaktihi shivasya pashuvartinī,*
> *Bandhayitrī svamārgasthā jñātā siddhyupapādikā.* [92]

Realizing that the same *kriyā shakti* of Shiva is a binding force in a bound soul and the path to Reality in a soul with right understanding is the way to reveal the Supreme Power.

A seeker masters the *shakti chakra* when he becomes aware, through stillness and oneness, that the undifferentiated *spanda* principle is everywhere.

---

91. Ibid., IV-14.
92. Ibid., IV-18.

366. In reality, the essence of knowledge takes three forms: In pain and pleasure, it is dual; in experiences and memories, it is both dual and nondual; and in the awareness of one's own Self, it is nondual. It becomes manifold according to a person's individual *spanda*, or vibration. The variations in the universe are infinite. Because of the glory of *spanda shakti*, everything appears to be different according to its qualities, actions, shape, activities, and changes. On the level of duality, differences among objects are measured by their rate of vibration rather than their essence. While contemplating the *spanda* principle, a person experiences the ebb and flow of the world as *idam*, objective, and *aham*, subjective. In the play of Shiva's immanent aspect, the experience of the limited "I" (*ahamtā*) predominates. In His transcendent aspect, the perfect "I" (*pūrnāhantā*) predominates.

367. Just as one's senses carry out their work through the power of the conscious Shakti, the experiencers who have become serene and pure obtain undifferentiated awareness through the power of the *spanda* principle. They become manifest and then merge once again. Therefore, they have the characteristics of Shiva and are Shiva.

368. *Tasmāt sarvamayo jīvaha sarva bhāva samudbhavāt.*

An individual is everywhere. He contains all feelings. The entire universe is his form.

For this reason, he has the awareness of unity. There are no sounds or meanings which are not Shiva.

Tat samvedana rūpena tādātmya pratipattitaha.

In this state of oneness, one experiences the unity of sounds and their meanings without any sense of differences.

Bhoktaiva bhogyabhāvena sadā sarvatra samsthitaha. [93]

The experiencer himself exists always and everywhere in the form of objective experience.

Shiva, the experiencer, is everywhere at all times as the
object of experience. That which is experienced is also the
experiencer.

Iti vā yasya samvittihi krīdātvena akhilam jagat,
Sa pashyan satatam yukto jivanmukto na samshayaha. [94]

He who regards the entire universe as the play of the
Universal Consciousness is Paramashiva and is
liberated while in the body.

If that awareness arises in the mind of a meditator, he
becomes identical to Shiva, merges in Him, and attains
supreme bliss. This is called *Shiva nirvāna dikshā* and gives rise
to the feeling that one is Supreme Shiva. This unwavering
awareness constitutes the knowledge of the Self. It makes
one enter the city of supreme bliss. This is called the arising
of pure knowledge (*vidyodaya nishyanda*).

369. Enlightened beings attach little importance to the dis-
parities and differences of the external world or to the favor-
able or unfavorable conditions in their lives. The outlook of
an enlightened being ignores disparity and focuses on the
inner *spanda* principle. An awakened being constantly experiences this *spanda* principle, but an ordinary person
perceives it only at the beginning and end of his life.

370. Unity is simply the state of not perceiving duality. This is
the knowledge of Shiva. This unity-awareness is also called

---

93. Ibid., III-2.
94. Ibid., III-3.

bindu. The abode of God's power, which is also called the mighty Shakti Kundalinī, is the Self. When Shiva joins with Shakti, He obtains the power to create. Therefore, Shakti is the mother of the universe. The entire universe is filled with this Supreme Shakti. Shakti is in the universe and the universe is in Shakti. Shakti is not different from the universe, just as the sun is not different from its light. This is the *spanda nirnaya* of Shaivism. It is the inner knowledge of the great beings as well as the sublime knowledge which redeems the world. A person who lacks knowledge is blind. Knowledge is vision, nectar, love, and bliss. It is the ecstasy of Shaivism.

371. *Yatra sthitam idam sarvam kāryam yasmāccha nirgatam,*
     Tasyānāvrita rūpatvān na nirodhosti kutrachit.[95]

     For Him, in whom the whole objective world is revealed and from whom it arises, no obstruction is possible, because of His unshrouded nature.

The effect, or the world of experienced objects (*prameya*), exists in an undifferentiated form within Shiva, who is the cause. Thus, Shiva is the substratum of awareness, which is of the nature of *spanda.* Through Him, the world manifests outwardly. Nothing can veil the true essence of the Supreme Reality.

372. Even in the state of worldliness, nothing veils the essential nature of the Supreme Reality, which is *Aham vimarsha,* or pure "I"-awareness. It is the state of unity. Because it is omnipotent, nothing anywhere can prevent it from flowing freely. It has inconceivable power to do or undo anything. It is also called Shiva.

---

95. Ibid., I-2.

Tava cha mahimā vāng manasayor[96] — "Your glory is beyond mind and speech." He is limitless and beyond imagination. He is the One in the many, filled with sweetness. He is sweeter than the sweetest and supremely auspicious. Although He has created the universe in His own being, He Himself is pure and taintless.

Pavitrānām pavitram yo mangalānām cha mangalam,
Daivatam devatānām cha bhūtānām yo'vyayaha pitā. [97]

He is purer than the pure. He is supremely auspicious. He is the Lord of all celestial beings and mortals. He is the indestructible father of all beings.

373. To manifest the universe, He flows through the currents of His infinite powers, yet remains perfect. Shakti Herself is the perfect state of Her Lord. His form is divine. He throbs with the awareness of *Pūrno'ham* — "I am perfect." Therefore, His nature is bliss.

Dik kāla kalanonmuktā deshoddeshā visheshinī,
Vyapadeshtum ashakyā sāvakathyā paramārthataha. [98]

He is beyond limitations of direction, time, and objects. He is beyond limitations of distance, both near and far. Because He cannot be the subject of either subtle or articulated speech, He is indescribable and can be experienced only from within.

Nāpi tarka pratishthanāt — "He cannot be confined to logic or reasoning." *Vitarka ātmajnānam*[99] — "Unwavering aware-

---

96. *Shiva Mahimna Stotram*, 1.
97. *Vishnusahasranam*, 10.
98. *Vijñāna Bhairava*, 14.
99. *Shiva Sūtras*, I-17.

ness [that 'I am Shiva'] constitutes the knowledge of the
the Self." This is called the state of Bhairavi, which is free
from the meshes of thought and the afflictions of doubt. This
state is the essential nature of Bhairava, or Shankara. It is
also called *Shiva avasthā*, the state of Shiva. In this state, both
the immanent and the transcendent coexist in unity. The
immanent aspect consists of the entire universe of matter
and conscious beings. The transcendent aspect is supremely
pure and changeless. Both aspects are His. He alone, in the
form of *spanda*, exists in His immanent aspect from Sadāshiva
to an ant or a blade of grass. This universe exists in an
undifferentiated form as an object of knowledge within *spanda
shakti*.

One of the five actions of Parameshwara is to manifest
through *spanda shakti* the universe, which is concealed within
Him in a seed form. This becomes the outer universe. The
Self of the universe exists in the form of the universe. This is
Paramashiva's independent play. If one has understanding,
one sees the world as the Lord. Without understanding, one
sees it merely as the world. Truly, the world is the divine play
of God's supreme bliss. There is only bliss, independence,
and perfection. The One is in one, and the same One is in
many. *Namah Shivāya!*

34
Vedānta

374. Vedānta is a true and sublime philosophy, the knowledge of which was produced when the sages churned the ocean of Truth. There is a saying: *Vedānta vākyeshu sadā ramantā khalu bhāgyavantā* — "One who constantly revels in the words of Vedānta is extremely fortunate."

Vedanta literally means "the end of the Vedas." Like the Vedas themselves, the words of Vedānta are great mantras and contain a lofty teaching. The question may arise, "What is the purpose of Vedānta?" Vedānta explains what true happiness is and awakens humanity. It puts cowardice to flight. It reveals the inner Truth. In essence, the purpose and doctrine of Vedānta are the cessation of all pain and the attainment of bliss.

What is the root of all pain? That is what we will consider now. *Ajñāna prabhavam sarvam*[100] — "Ignorance is the root cause of all suffering." *Svasvarūpa vismarana* — "It is also the forgetfulness of one's own Self." Not to know one's own Self is ignorance. A human being's predicament is that he has

---

100. Shankārachārya, *Aparokshānubhūti*, 17.

forgotten himself. He thinks about others and dwells on their faults, wasting the priceless years of his life by uselessly envying and criticizing others. What greater ignorance can there be? Ignorance is the city of utter darkness. Unless a person transcends it, he cannot find perfect contentment.

Notpadyate vina jnanam vicharenanya sadhanaihi,
Yatha padarthabhanam hi prakashena vina kvachit. [101]

Just as objects cannot be seen without light, one cannot attain knowledge except through contemplation of the Self.

One should contemplate only the Self. Instead of looking at external objects, one should turn within and contemplate the Self by means of the mind. Self-inquiry should be as follows:

Ko'ham kathamidam jatam ko vai kartasya vidyate,
Upadanam kimastiha vicharaha so'yamidrishaha. [102]

Who am I? How did this world come into existence? Who is its creator? What is the material cause of the world?

In reality, the world exists only in our imagination. Suppose that a rope is lying on the ground and we see it as a snake and become afraid. There was never a snake in the rope. The snake appeared because of an optical illusion, a delusion on the part of the observer. In this way, we fear our own imaginary snake and become the cause of our own pain or pleasure.

Ajnana prabhavam sarvam jnanena praviliyate[103] — "Everything is produced by ignorance and dissolves in the wake of

---

101. Ibid., 11.
102. Ibid., 12.
103. Ibid., 17.

knowledge." All pain, disappointment, weakness, mental disturbance, jealousy, enmity, envy, and so on, are the progeny of ignorance. These things which make a person unhappy are destroyed through knowledge. Ignorance arises from various mental constructs, and only knowledge can counteract it. The world of thoughts is the source of one's pain. This is what Vedānta states.

What is the purpose of Vedānta? This is the primary question. Its purpose is to put an end to all pain forever and to enable us to attain supreme bliss. Once this bliss is attained, it can never be destroyed. A person may ask, "Even if all pain goes away, can it not return? Even if supreme bliss is attained, can it not be destroyed?" However, the real teaching of Vedānta is that the ignorance which is destroyed never really existed. To destroy ignorance and attain bliss is to destroy what never was and to attain what we have always had. Therefore, ignorance is not valid because it is merely a figment of our imagination; we should discard it through proper understanding. The Self of all, which is extremely subtle, is forever attained. Because of ignorance, we do not see it; therefore, we think we have not attained it. Since it is already ours, we attain what was already attained. *Ātmā tu satatam prāptau* — "The Self is already attained."

> *Vāyunānīyate meghaha punas tenaiva nīyate,*
> *Manasā kalpyate bandho mokshas tenaiva kalpyate.*
>
> Clouds come into being because of the wind and vanish because of the wind. Similarly, the mind is responsible for bondage as well as liberation.

375. Actually bondage is not real. Shaivism declares it to be the glory of *mātrikā shakti*. Once the creations of the mind dissolve, the idea of liberation also vanishes. Then the true Principle is just as it always was, perfect and unchanging. Enlightened beings have divided the world of names, forms,

and objects into three kinds of reality: *prātibhāsika sattā*, the apparent reality of the dream state; *vyāvahārika sattā*, the reality of the waking state; and *pāramārthika sattā*, Absolute Reality.

As long as delusion exists, dreams appear. This is *prāti-bhāsika sattā*. Once the delusion is destroyed, that reality also vanishes. That which appears empirically at one time and not another — just as the *Guru Gītā* is chanted only in the morning and not at night — is *vyāvahārika sattā*, the reality of the waking state. The One who is experienced through knowledge as the Self of all in the continual play of Consciousness is *pāramārthika sattā*. That is also called the true Self, Brahman, one's own true nature, and the Absolute Reality. That One is experienced in the state of equanimity, or *samādhi*. It is the awareness of the Self of all.

> *Sadidam paramādvaitam svas*
> *mād anyasya vastuna' bhāvān,*
> *Na hyanyad asti kinchit samyak*
> *paramārtha tattva bodhe hi.* [104]

In reality, only total unity, which is the embodiment of supreme bliss, is the true Principle. There is nothing other than the Self. Once a person has the knowledge of the Principle of the Self, there is no longer any other.

Sad brahmakārya sakalam sadaiva — "The entire world, which is the effect of the true Brahman, is made of His own nature." Because the effect is not separate from the cause, the world is the play of Brahman. Anyone who says that the world is different from God is still ignorant. His speech is nonsense, like that of a person who is dreaming. Vedānta says, *Sarvam khalvidam brahma* — "Everything is Brahman."

---

104. Shankārachārya, *Viveka Chudāmani*, 226.

Everything is real; nothing is different from Consciousness. Just as emptiness is full of space and cloth is permeated by thread, Brahman pervades the entire world. Just as liquidity is in water as water, light is in a flame as the flame, fragrance is in camphor as camphor, activity is inherent in the body, and gold is in both nuggets and ornaments, similarly, the Knower, God, or Brahman is the primordial cause of the entire world, and His image appears in all. When a stream twists and winds, the water also appears to be crooked, although in reality it is not. When iron is heated it looks red, but the redness belongs to the fire, not to the iron. In the same way, the principle of Consciousness appears as the world because of the deception created by ignorance, but that Consciousness never becomes ignorant.

Brahman, or Consciousness, appears as the mind, senses, *gunas*, and other principles. However, just as sweetness does not depend on the shape of the sweets, Brahman does not depend on the *gunas*, *sattva*, *rajas*, and *tamas*. Just as *ghee* is in milk but is not milk, the entire world is in Brahman yet is not Brahman. In this way, we should clearly understand that Brahman is different from the senses and their *gunas*. All words, names, forms, relationships, and activities are related to the world of forms, not to Brahman. Brahman cannot be the *gunas*; the *gunas* are reflected in Him. An ignorant person thinks that the *gunas* are one with Brahman. This kind of understanding is as deluded as saying that the sky is one with the clouds, a mirror is one with its reflections, or water is one with the sun that it reflects. Likewise, it is useless to say that Brahman contains *gunas*. There is actually no relationship between Brahman and *gunas*. When a beggar dreams that he is a king and enjoys sense pleasures, it is unreal, a mere dream. Similarly, to think that the formless Brahman experiences *gunas* is nothing but delusion. The *gunas* experience themselves. The *gunas* in the form of the senses move among the *gunas* in the form of sense objects. The *gunas* are under the control of the Supreme Reality and carry out their respective functions. All actions take place under the direction of the Supreme Principle.

376. Although sparks of fire are of different sizes, their heat is the same. Similarly, the same Brahman pervades in His fullness all sentient beings and insentient objects. In this way, the indestructible One permeates everything in a subtle form. We should come to know Him. He is inside as well as outside the body. He is both near and far. He is the One without a second.

In the ocean of milk,[105] the sweetness is no greater in the middle than near the shore. In the same way, the One who is all-pervasive and perfect completely pervades all the various beings and creatures, those born of egg, sweat, seed, and womb. O seekers! The moon may be reflected in thousands of pots, yet it is only one. Although there are countless grains of salt, they all share the same quality of saltiness. The same sweetness exists in different pieces of sugarcane. The One has become both matter and consciousness, both movable and immovable things, yet remains different from all.

Bahirantashcha bhūtānām acharāmcharameva cha[106] — "The One pervades all beings, inside and outside, movable and immovable." *Avibhaktam cha bhuteshu vibhaktamiva cha sthitam*[107] — "In creatures, He is undivided although He appears to be divided." In this way, the One who pervades all equally and who is the primordial cause of the creation of the universe has created all beings and is the substratum of them all. Just as the body is the basis of childhood, maturity, and old age, that One is the basis of the three processes of

---

105. A legendary ocean, described in the Puranas, which the gods and demons churned in order to extract various divine gifts.

106. *Bhagavad Gītā*, XIII-15.

107. Ibid.

creation, preservation, and dissolution. Just as the sky remains unaffected by the passing of morning, noon, and night, Consciousness remains unaffected by these processes. The One is called Brahmā during creation, Vishnu during preservation, Rudra during dissolution, and Consciousness when these three processes have ceased. Consciousness swallows the great void of the ether and remains as the witness of the void. It is the Knower of all.

Jyotishāmapi tajjyotihi — "That Supreme Principle is the light of all lights." It is the nectar of the moon and the brilliance of the sun. Receiving light from Consciousness, the stars twinkle. The Supreme Principle is the Supreme brilliance of the sun. The Supreme Principle is the Supreme Light. It is the fundamental cause of everything in the universe. It is the intellect of the intellect, the *prāna* of the *prāna*, the mind of the mind, the eye of the eye, the ear of the ear, the speech of speech, the movement of movement.

377. The creation of forms, their expansion, preservation, and destruction all proceed from That. That supports the earth through its own power. It is the essence of water. Light exists because of that Principle. It is the power behind the movement of the wind, and because of it, the ether is everywhere. We should come to know that Supreme Principle. It has not the slightest trace of duality. By perceiving it, the seer, the process of seeing, and the seen merge together. When *sādhanā* and its goal become one, the knowledge of Brahman dawns. Brahman is that which is known. When counting ceases, numbers are of equal value; they are all composed of ones. Similarly, once Brahman is attained, the concepts of both the means and the end vanish.

Hridi sarvasya vishtitam. [108] The same Parabrahman exists eternally in the hearts of all. One who sees no differences

---

108. Ibid., XIII-17.

among all existing creatures attains the bliss of Parabrahman in this very body. Although thousands of lamps may be blazing, the light in all of them is the same.

Samam pashyanhi sarvatra[109] — "He sees God equally everywhere." If a person leads his life seeing God and all beings as identical, he becomes liberated in this lifetime. He does not get caught on the wheel of birth and death. With this wisdom of equality and oneness, he sleeps comfortably in a bed of bliss and fearlessness. Such a person is fortunate. He is a great seeker. He becomes a supreme yogi as well as a Siddha.

Sharīrasthopi kaunteya na karoti na lipyate[110] — "O Arjuna! Although He lives in the body, He neither does anything nor is touched by anything." Although the sun is reflected in water, it remains detached from it. Similarly, although God dwells in the body, He remains supremely pure. Most ignorant people commit a grave error by considering themselves to be sinners. When the pure Self constantly dwells within them, how can they be sinners? The body is the divine temple of God, who resides in the heart. If you wish to find Him, seek Him in your heart. *Hridi sannivishtam* — "He lives in the heart."

378. Ignorant people consider the reflection of the sun in water to be the sun. But the sun is unchanging. It exists before the water appears and after it vanishes. Similarly, although it is correct to say that the Self is in the body, still, it existed before the body came into being and will continue to exist after the body dies. Just as our own faces can be seen in a mirror, so the Self exists in the body. The Self is neither the doer nor the nondoer. It is neither thin nor fat. It is neither visible nor invisible. It is neither lustrous nor dull. The true

---

109. Ibid., XIII-28.
110. Ibid., XIII-31.

nature of the Self is supreme bliss, not sorrow. The Self always remains as it is. Just as day and night come and go in the heavens, similarly, countless bodies come and go in the Self. However, the Self always remains detached from those bodies. The Self is everywhere in all bodies, but it is never attached to bodily actions.

379. The Supreme Principle is the Self which transcends the pervasiveness of ether. It is on the opposite shore from the material world, where there is no distinction between unity and disparity. In that place, all forms disappear, individual existence is extinguished, and there are neither nightmares nor phantoms. That is the resting place of the Self. Yogis and enlightened beings rest in that perfect bliss.

Only those who have received the grace of the Guru and are adept at discriminating between the Self and the non-Self can grasp the Supreme Principle. One who has merged into the Guru, the embodiment of wisdom, who has become him, who has merged into the all-pervasive Consciousness, who has become both immanent and transcendent, who has lost his sense of duality, and who has become ecstatic in supreme bliss and complete in his perfection dwells in all and all dwell in him. He is God incarnate. He is the Consciousness of Consciousness. Such an enlightened being is blessed. He is God walking and speaking in the form of a human being.

35

Pratyabhijñāsāra: The Essence of the Doctrine of Recognition

380. A great Siddha, Kshemarāja, summarized the *Pratyabhijñā* philosophy. His book, the *Pratyabhijñāhridayam*, contains only twenty aphorisms, but it is not just a small book; it is a sublime philosophy. It is easy even for ordinary people to understand, but easiest for those who have received the grace of *shaktipāt* from God or from the Guru.

Shaktipātonmishita parameshwara samāveshā bhilāshinaha[111] — "For those who aspire to it, *samavesha*, or mergence with Shiva, blossoms with the descent of Shakti." *Shaktipāt* is the compassionate will of Paramashiva; it is also called grace. *Shaktipāt* received from the Guru or from God inspires us to walk on the path of Self-knowledge. The compassion of Paramashiva, the Guru, takes the form of *shaktipāt*. The *Shiva Sūtra Vimarshinī* says, *Gururvā parameshwarī anugrāhikā shaktihi* — "The Guru is the grace-bestowing power of God." *Shaktipāt* is given so that one can experience one's own Self. *Shaktipāt* is described in the Vedas, the Upanishads, the Tantras, and other scriptures.

The *Pratyabhijñāhridayam* begins by describing Chiti, God's power which is inseparable from Him, and ends with a description of the state of Chiti. The first aphorism is *Chitihi*

---

111. Kshemarāja, *Pratyabhijñāhridayam*, commentary on 1.

svatantrā vishva siddhi hethuhu — "Supremely independent Chiti is the cause of the [manifestation, maintenance, and reabsorption of the] universe." Chiti is the glorious Parāshakti who is the cause of all the principles from Sadāshiva to the earth. She is the origin of the universe. She also causes one to repose in Paramashiva and to merge into Him.

381. The expansion of the world of sentient beings and insentient objects is the doing of Chiti. Although Chiti Herself creates the world, sustains it, and finally merges it into Herself, nothing can limit Her true nature. It is an established truth that Chiti is all-pervasive, ever-blissful, and perfect. She is the primordial mother of the universe.

> *Grāhya grāhaka samvittihi sāmānya sarvadehinām.* [112]
>
> Both *grāhya*, the seen, and *grāhaka*, the seer, are the Universal Consciousness.

Abhinavagupta states:

> *Evam desha kālā sparshāt vibhutvam cha sakala,*
> *Desha kālāsparsho'pi tannirmāna yogāt-iti tato'pi*
> *vyāpakatva nityattve.*
>
> She is beyond the limits of space and time, and She is all-pervasive and eternal. The limitations of space and time are the effects of Her creation.

She transcends both of them. Therefore, She is also called the Sublime Reality, the Great Goddess, and the Mother of the Universe. This same Chiti is the Mahā Kundalinī. She is of the nature of Parabrahman. Through Her grace alone, the spontaneous Kriyā Yoga, also known as Mahā Yoga or Siddha Yoga, takes place. Kundalinī Chiti Shakti carries one who loves the Guru and has done *sādhanā* to the *sahasrāra* and

---

112. *Vijñāna Bhairava*, 107.

merges that person in Shiva. Chiti Herself takes on a human form to become the Guru and carry out the function of *shaktipāt*. Through the power of Chiti alone, the universe is created and destroyed.

382.   *Svecchayā svabhittau vishvam unmīlayati.* [113]

Of Her own free will, Chiti unfolds the universe on Her own screen.

Chiti, through Her own will, manifests the universe. Without depending on anything else for support, She manifests the universe of duality on Her own being. Like a city reflected in a mirror, that universe is inseparable from Her.

383.   *Tan nānā anurūpa grāhya grāhaka bhedāt.* [114]

That universe is manifold because of the differentiation of reciprocally adapted objects and subjects.

As Consciousness contracts, it takes the form of the universe. Although it is contracted, Consciousness still exists in its fullness. As it descends from its natural state of limitlessness, it contracts and becomes the objects perceived. Then it is called *chitta*, the mind. In reality, the mind is nothing but the Goddess Chiti Herself. As She contracts, She conceals Her true nature. Chiti also becomes *māyā pramātā*, the individual soul governed by *māyā*. The *Shiva Sūtras* say, *Ātmā chittam* [115] — "The individual Self is mind." It becomes the mind when *jñāna shakti*, the power of knowledge, is limited.

384.   Although Chiti is one, She becomes twofold, threefold, fourfold, and of the nature of seven pentads (groups of five)

113. Kshemarāja, *Pratyabhijñāhridayam*, 2.

114. Ibid., 3.

115. *Shiva Sūtras*, III-2.

with their thirty-five principles.[116] Then She is called a limited, transmigratory individual.

385. All philosophers speak of the same One according to their own languages and opinions.

386. When the Shakti of the Self contracts, She is known as a limited individual, subject to innumerable births and deaths. She remains a transmigratory soul as long as She is contracted, but once She expands, She becomes Paramashiva.

387. In Her contracted form, She is called the mind, but when the mind turns within and ascends to the status of Universal Consciousness, She is once again called Chiti. When one experiences this expanded state, one has the knowledge of universality. When Chiti becomes objects, She is the mind, and when She becomes the Self, She is Chiti.

388. This is why it is essential for everyone to meditate. When the mind turns within in meditation, it becomes the light of Consciousness. Meditation is sublime alchemy. It is a mighty power which annihilates all pain. It is the seed mantra of humanity's glory. Meditation has the power to make a human being become the Lord, an individual become Shiva, and the soul become God. *Na hi dhyānāt parā sādhanā* — "There is no *sādhanā* higher than meditation." There is no mantra higher than meditation. There is no power higher than meditation. When we attain the power of the Self, we become one with the universe. In reality, the universe is not

---

116. Twofold: the experiencer and the object of experience; threefold: the three *malas*, or impurities (*āṇava mala, māyīya mala, kārma mala*); fourfold: the void (*shūnya*), the vital force (*prāṇa*), the subtle body (*puryashtaka*), and the gross body (*sharīra*). For seven pentads, see Glossary.

different from us, nor are we different from the universe. If anyone were to ask me what the universe is, I would say, "The universe is me."

389. Once a person attains the bliss of Consciousness, although bodily awareness remains, he firmly perceives the Self as Consciousness. This is liberation while in the body and the supreme means of attaining bliss.

390. When the central *nādī* unfolds, one attains the bliss of Consciousness. The Kundalinī lies at the base of the *sushumnā*, or central *nādī*. Through the Guru's grace, she is awakened, and one spontaneously attains the bliss of Consciousness. Kundalinī, the supreme deity, is the embodiment of absolute bliss. Once She is awakened, how can one not be blissful? The entire world is full of bliss. When this mighty Shakti is awakened, She permeates the whole body and remolds a person in the image of supreme bliss.

391. By the unfoldment of the central *nādī*, one attains the bliss of Consciousness, which is the *samādhi* of yogis. Supreme bliss is the highest *samādhi*. The essence of the perfect "I"-consciousness is light and bliss. It is nothing but the power of the great mantra. By entering that perfect "I"-consciousness, a person attains mastery over his group of deities of Consciousness. These deities bring about the creation, sustenance, and reabsorption of the universe. This means that a person becomes God by merging into Him. He is God and becomes God. Even if he is not aware of it, he is still God. Muktānanda says, "What exists without God? What is not God? If you have found Him, you have found Him. But even if you think you have not found Him, you have found Him. Nothing exists without Shiva."

36

The Vijñāna Bhairava

392.   The *Vijñāna Bhairava* is an Āgama. It is a text revealed by God and written in the form of questions and answers between Goddess Bhairavi and Lord Bhairava. Its fundamental teaching is the identity of Shiva and Shakti.

This divine work is incomparably great. Philosophical texts quote from the *Vijñāna Bhairava*. It is also used as an authoritative reference in other writings. The *Vijñāna Bhairava* is not only a great and universal work of literature, but the wisdom of Bhairava Himself. It is the wisdom of His own Self. It partakes of the true nature of the Supreme Principle, Vijñāna Bhairava.[117]

393.   Replying to the questions of the Goddess, Lord Shiva says, "Just as articles produced by a magician, things created by *māyā*, and objects seen in a dream have no real existence, the Lord's manifestation in *sakala* form does not really exist." *Sakala* means that which is perceived by the senses, mind, and intellect. Everything from Brahmā to an insect is referred to as *sakala*; Lord Shiva transcends all these things. In

---

117. Paramashiva.

the scriptures, *sakala* is explained in detail for the sake of ignorant people who take interest in the deceptive objects of illusion. It is also said that the nature of *sakala* is described in the scriptures to prevent the ignorant from heading in the wrong direction. These descriptions encourage them to engage in mantra repetition, worship, prayer, and other spiritual practices in order to become virtuous. After they have consistently performed these good actions and obtained the grace of the Supreme Guru, they may experience *nishkala*, transcendental Consciousness.

It is impossible to describe the transcendental nature of Lord Bhairava. His true and essential nature is *nirvikalpa bodha svarūpa* — transcendental wisdom, or changeless awareness. It can be experienced only within. The entire universe is His play. In such a state, where there is nothing other than the Supreme Reality, who worships whom? Who bestows grace on whom? The supreme nature of Lord Bhairava is also the nature of Parādevi. Like fire and its heat, they are inseparable.

Na vahner dāhikā shaktihi vyatiriktā vibhāvyate,
Kevalam jñāna sattāyām prārambho'yam praveshane. [118]

The burning power of fire is not different from fire. One finds this to be true even after pondering it deeply. It is described as separate only for the sake of the listener as a preliminary step toward knowing it.

Parāshakti can never be different from Her Lord, Bhairava. Shakti makes one recognize His true existence. She is the primary means of experiencing His nature.

394. Just as fire and its heat are not different, the wisdom of Bhairava and Parāshakti are not separate. Just as fire is felt through heat, Shiva can be understood through the assis-

---

118. *Vijñāna Bhairava*, 19.

tance of Parāshakti. Parāshakti is the door by which one reaches Shiva. Just as we can recognize a person by his face, similarly, we recognize the essential nature of Shiva by coming to know Parāshakti. Just as through the light of the sun or of a flame we can see in all directions, in the same way, the knowledge of Shiva is acquired through Shakti.

395. After Lord Bhairava has explained this, the Goddess asks Him how to attain this Supreme Principle. In answer, Lord Shiva describes 112 *dharanas*, or centering techniques.

In this work, Parāshakti, Chiti Shakti, Kundalinī, and Mahā Shakti are all synonymous. The Lord's essential nature in the state of unity is called Kāli or Shakti, and in the state of duality it is called *prāna shakti*. *Prāksamvitti prāne parinatā* — "The Universal Consciousness itself becomes *prāna*." It has become the five *prānas* (*prāna, apāna*, and so on) and permeates the body in order to make it function. In fact, as *sādhanā* unfolds, three things come together in the vibration of the *prāna shakti*: the power of God, the power of the individual, and the individual's own effort. By merging the mind into the vibrating *prāna shakti* in the heart region, one attains the supreme state.

Actually it is impossible to merge into one's own Self because there is no reality other than the essential nature of the Self to merge with. Nor are the *upāyas* different from That. Therefore, the entire world is the essence of Consciousness.

Etasamajjāyate prāno manaha sarvendriyāni cha,
Kham vāyur jyotir āpaha prithivī vishvasya dhārinī.[119]

From Consciousness emanates everything: the *prāna*, the mind, all the senses, ether, air, light (fire), water, and earth, the supporter of all.

---

119. *Mundaka Upanishad*, II-1-3.

Time cannot grasp it; space cannot divide it; limitations cannot bind it. It has no form. It cannot be comprehended through words. *Napi pramāna gocharāt* — "It cannot be understood through any *pramānas*" (means of knowledge such as direct perception, inference, or scriptural authority). This essential and true nature of the Self, which is independent and blissful, of its own accord gives forms to all the above-mentioned principles ranging from time to various *pramānas*. The entire universe is reflected in the pure "I"-consciousness of the Self and in the awareness "I am not different from the true Self." When this inner understanding is awakened in a seeker, he merges into the essential nature of the eternal God. There is no need for mantra repetition, worship, meditation, *āratī*, and so on. These practices purify the psyche and the mind and make a person worthy by increasing the subtlety of his intellect. However, the Supreme Principle, which is the wisdom of Bhairava, is self-luminous and eternal. It is inside and outside everyone.

> *Antar bahischcha tat sarvam*
> *vyāpya nārāyanah sthitaha.* [120]

Lord Nārāyana [Bhairava] exists pervading and penetrating, within and without, everything which is perceived in the universe.

Whether one goes to the middle of the ocean or stays close to the shore, there is water. In the same way, the wisdom of Bhairava exists wherever one goes, wherever one looks, however one eats, drinks, plays, laughs, or cries, and whatever one does. He sees all, knows all, experiences all, and sheds light on all. How could the poor eyes see without Bhairava? How could the poor ears hear without Him? Without the Self, could the cleverness of the fleshly tongue do

---

120. *Nārāyana Upanishad*, X-90.

anything with its net of words? How could the nose take interest in fragrance without His help?

Vijñāna Bodha Bhairava is also called Paramashiva. What words can I write to describe Him? Without Him, would the *prāna* and *apāna*, the inhalation and exhalation, flow in and out ceaselessly day and night? Bhairava utters the syllable *ham* with the *apāna* and *so* with the *prāna* and exists in the junction point between them. He digests all food. He makes the blood circulate throughout the body. Everything is in Him and belongs to Him. He is everything. Bhairava knows everything, everywhere, at all times. No one can know Him, for He is the Knower of all. *Sve mahimni sthitaha* — "He exists in His own glory." He has eyes which see the entire world, but our eyes cannot see Him. A seeker is very fortunate if he can attain the vision of Him through the Guru's grace.

> *Upāya jālam na shivam prakāshayed*
> *ghatena kim bhāti sahasra dīdhitihi;*
> *Vivechayan nittha mudāra darshanaha*
> *svayam prakāsham shiva māvishet kshanāt.*[121]

No mundane means can reveal Shiva. Can an inert clay pot illumine the shining sun? A being whose vision has expanded and who contemplates in this way merges into the essential nature of the self-luminous Shiva within.

The *Samvit Prakāsha* says:

> *Aparokshe bhavat tattve sarvataha prakate sthite,*
> *Yairupāyāhā pratanyante nūnam tvām na vidanti te.*

Your nature and essence are manifest before the eyes of all. Even though this is so, if a person employs different means to see You, then it is certain that he does not know You.

---

121. Abhinavagupta, *Tantrāsāra*.

Everyone already perceives the essential nature of Vijnāna Bhairava, the Self. The world would not exist without Him. Realizing this, a seeker becomes established in his own true nature and becomes the Self of the universe, for he was that Self all along.

396. The basis of *prāna* and *apāna* is the space of the inner *dvādashānta*, or inner heart, and the space of the outer *dvādashānta*, or outer heart. In these spaces, the activity of *prāna* and *apāna* ceases for a moment. For a fraction of a second, they "turn within" as *ham*, the sound of the inhalation, merges inside and *so*, the sound of the exhalation, merges outside. At that moment, one feels as though *prāna* and *apāna* have vanished somewhere. This space where they merge is called *madhyadashā*. When it expands, one's vision of duality and one's feeling that others are different from oneself are gradually reduced. Eventually both one's outer and inner senses turn within completely.

397. *Madhya vikāsāt chidānanda lābhaha*[122] — "By the unfoldment of the center, there is acquisition of the bliss of Consciousness." The central *nādi* is Bhairavi. She is the face of Shiva. She is the primordial Shakti of all human beings and of the entire world. Everything is Her doing. Bondage and liberation, pain and pleasure, high and low, honor and dishonor, poverty and wealth, knowledge and ignorance, supreme bliss and utter dryness are all the play of Shakti. When the Shakti is awakened in the space of the *madhyadashā* and turns within, the movement of the *prāna* gradually merges into the *sushumnā*, the central *nādi*. Then the real nature of Lord Bhairava is revealed by Parashākti Bhairavi. He is inseparable from Her.

---

122. Kshemarāja, *Pratyabhijñāhridayam*, 17.

Prāna moves in the heart, the throat, the palate, the forehead, the *brahmarandhra* at the crown of the head, and the *dvādashānta*. If even for a moment the *prāna* dissolves in one of these locations and the *apāna* does not arise, then outer *kumbhaka*, or retention of breath, occurs effortlessly. Similarly, if the *apāna* dissolves for a moment in one of these locations and the *prāna* does not arise, then inner *kumbhaka* occurs. The space of *madhyadashā* is called the supreme state. Only a yogi or an enlightened being knows the *madhyadashā* between the *prāna* and *apāna*. If a yogi turns inward even for a moment, the *madhyadashā* expands within him and the *prāna* and *apāna* cease. The *Vijñāna Bhairava* says that he then becomes liberated.

398. To eliminate all doubts, Bhairava answers the questions of the Goddess and explains that supreme and true Principle which is fully experienced by all the great sages, ascetics, enlightened beings, and yogis.

O Bhairavi, Mahā Shakti, primordial seed of the world! You are blessed. You are worthy of honor and worship. Listen. Now Bhairava is going to give the supremely secret answer to Your question. O Parabhairavi! The Supreme Principle, Consciousness, Satchidānanda is worthy of reverence. He is the ultimate Lord of all and is worshipped in all religions as the supreme deity. He bestows grace according to a devotee's desire. The supreme state of this ancient Bhairava cannot be confined to different directions such as east and west or limited to the present moment or any other time. It is referred to as being both near and far. Although it is described in these terms, no adjective applies to it. We cannot limit it by describing it or referring to it in terms of space or time. It is difficult to understand its nature because it neither vibrates in *madhyamā*, the subtle level of speech, nor can it be expressed in *vaikharī*, articulated speech. Because the essential nature of the supreme state cannot be divided by space, time, name, form, and so on, it is very difficult to come to know it through language.

When the perfect "I"-consciousness unfolds within, it is experienced as spontaneously surging bliss. This perfect "I"-consciousness unfolds when grace is received in the form of *shaktipāt*. Because its nature is totally free of all momentary fantasies, names, forms, and other limitations, it is *nirvikalpa*, free of thoughts and modifications. This is the Truth. This state is the essential nature of the wisdom of Bhairava. It pervades the entire universe as *aham*. It is also reflected on the pure screen of one's own Self. It is not concealed by the impurities of the world. It illumines the entire universe. The Lord's *nishkala*, or transcendental nature, is revealed in this supreme state. It has no form other than the experience of bliss.

399. After discussing the nature of the Supreme, Bhairava once again emphasizes the futility of rituals and the objects associated with them. In the transcendental state, the state of Parabhairava or "I"-consciousness, who is there to perform worship? Who will be propitiated by that worship? For a seeker, there is nothing else to worship or offer except the essential nature of his own Self. The worship, the worshipper, the object of worship, and so on, are merely different aspects of the Supreme Principle. Its divine nature is Consciousness and bliss. When this is the case, all actions are futile compared to knowledge of the Self.

> *Shakti shaktimator yadvad*
> *abhedaha sarvadā sthitaha,*
> *Atas tad dharma dharmitvāt*
> *parāshaktihi parātmanaha.* [123]

---

123. *Vijñāna Bhairava*, 18.

It is certain that Shakti, the essential nature of Bhairava, is inseparable from Bhairava, the supreme state.

Shakti is power. This power is the true nature of Bhairava, who has created the entire world. Shakti and Her Lord are inseparable. The Shakti is called Bhairavi since She is associated with Bhairava and also with such qualities as omniscience, omnipotence, and omnipresence. She is not different from the Self, which is a mass of Consciousness and bliss.

Shaktyā vinā shive sūkshme nām dhāma na vidyate.

Because Shiva is very subtle, He cannot be known without Shakti.

The essential point of the *Vijñāna Bhairava* is that one can perceive the identical nature of Shakti and Shiva only with the help of Parāshakti. Therefore, the Siddhas emphasize the need for *shaktipāt*, the awakening of the Shakti, and its unfoldment. *Shaktipāt* itself is Shakti. The entire world arises from Shiva just as a seed sprouts. A seed sprouts spontaneously when it is combined with such factors as soil and water. In the same way, when the Shakti is awakened through *shaktipāt* and the Guru's grace, the Shakti increases on Her own and makes a person one with Shiva. This Shakti is described as follows: *Sā sphurattā mahā sattā* — "She is the great vibrating Reality." She transforms Shiva into the world, and in the same way She transforms the individual soul into Shiva. She is also called the *spanda* principle.

400.   What does the *Vijñāna Bhairava* teach us?

Nijadehe sarvadikkam yugapad bhāvayed viyat,
Nirvikalpa manās tasya viyat sarvam pravartate.[124]

---

124. Ibid., 63.

If a person contemplates empty space both in his body and in all directions simultaneously, without any thoughts, he experiences empty space all around him and identifies with the vast expanse of Consciousness.

A seeker should become one-pointed and free of thoughts. He should feel the all-pervasive Consciousness everywhere. He should feel it simultaneously (not sequentially) in the east, west, north, and south as well as in his body. By practicing this awareness, he attains knowledge of the true state. As the feeling that the visible world is the Void, or Consciousness, becomes firmer, his own essential nature, the true Principle, is revealed. *Bhāve hi vidyate devo* — "God exists in the power of feeling." In Mahārāshtra lived the great yoginī Bahinābāi, who said, *Bahinī mhane bhāva icchā phaladāyinī* — "One's feeling yields the fruit of one's own desire." Therefore, one should meditate with firm feeling.

401. O beautiful one! A yogi merges his inner and outer senses, such as the mind and the eyes, into the sublime space which arises in the heart. This is the center of *prāna* and *apāna*. Through his own feeling, he enters the center of the two bowls of the heart lotus and becomes established there in his own true nature. The upper bowl of the heart lotus represents knowledge; the lower bowl represents objects. The center of the heart lotus represents Consciousness, or the Knower. Therefore, a yogi who fixes his mind on Consciousness and engages it in nothing else attains the state of infinite bliss when the ecstasy of the grandeur of the Lord of the universe unfolds.

402. *Sarvatah sva sharīrasya dvādashānte mano layāt,*
Dridha buddher dridhībhūtam tattva lakshyam pravartate. [125]

---

125. Ibid., 50.

A yogi experiences Reality when all parts of his body are penetrated by Consciousness and when his mind, which has become firm through one-pointedness, dissolves in the inner *dvādashānta*.

The central *nādī*, or *sushumnā*, is also known as the *dvādashānta*. A yogi merges into the sublime, thought-free state when the Deity of Consciousness enters every pore of his body as the light of the Kundalinī which has been awakened in the central *nādī*. By merging into the *dvādashānta*, the space where the breath dissolves, all the impressions of the yogi's mind are weakened, his mind becomes more one-pointed, and he continues to progress steadily. Finally, he reaches the state of repose in the Self.

403. This pure knowledge of Consciousness arises naturally. A seeker or a yogi should focus this knowledge on any one of the previously mentioned locations. At every moment, again and again, he should try to make the mind one-pointed there. When he does this, the tendencies of his mind become calm, and he soon attains the unique inner knowledge of Bhairava. This is a centering technique. Perfection is only a dream without meditation and a centering technique. The *Vijñāna Bhairava* says that meditation and the practice of centering techniques are impossible without the inner awakening.

404. *Īdrishena kramenaiva yatra kutrāpi chintanā,*
Shūnye kudye pare pātre svayam līnā varapradā. [126]

In this way, whenever one concentrates in successive steps on empty space, a wall, or a noble person,

---

126. Ibid., 33.

that concentration is absorbed by itself into the supreme and grants the highest spiritual experience.

One should practice focusing on the *mūlādhāra* at the base of the spine, the womb (*janma*), the sacral plexus (*kanda*), the navel, the heart, the throat, the palate, the space between the eyebrows, the forehead, the *brahmarandhra* in the crown of the head, and Shakti, either in successive stages or singly. Besides the body, one can also focus on empty space, a noble person, or a being who has a pure mind. *Vītarāga vishayam vā chittam*[127] — "Focus the mind on a being who has risen above passion and attachment." When a seeker practices these techniques steadfastly day and night, when he remembers and contemplates a being whose attachment and aversion have been destroyed, his mind merges spontaneously into the Self, and he has the highest spiritual experience. These techniques bring the sublime experience of the Supreme Light blazing forth.

Sarvottūrna rūpam sopāna padakramena samshrayataha,
Paratattva rūdhi lābhe paryante shivamayī bhāvaha. [128]

By climbing step by step, the yogi reaches the highest stage of oneness with Shiva.

The sacral plexus, the navel, the heart, the throat, the subtle principles of *bindu* and *nāda*, and Shakti all function as steps to the Supreme Principle. When a person climbs steps, he leaves each one behind as he proceeds to the next until he reaches his destination. In the same way, a yogi leaves one stage behind when he proceeds to another until he finally reaches the highest and most exalted state of all. Then he himself becomes Shiva.

---

127. *Patanjali Yoga Sūtras*, I-37.
128. *Paramārthasāra.*

Identification with unity arises by reflecting on the supreme state and by merging into one's own Self with the awareness "I am That." Having this recognition of the Self is the basis for right identification. This matter is explained in the *Spanda Kārikā*:

> *Yasmāt sarvamayo jīvaha sarva bhāva samudbhavāt,*
> *Tat samvedana rūpena tādātmya pratipattitaha.* [129]

> The individual soul is identical with the whole universe because the origin of all things is attributed to him and because he attains universality through his knowledge of the whole.

The individual is everything. He is identical with the universe because he is the knower of all objects and all objects take birth from him. He, as the knower, is one with both knowledge and the means of knowing. In the state of oneness, the universe of sound (i.e., Consciousness vibrating as sound) and the universe of matter are not different. There is no state which is not illumined by Consciousness, the nature of Shiva. From this, it becomes very clear that the nature of Shiva, or Consciousness, which is light, is also revealed as the known. Therefore, from our own experience, we can say unhesitatingly that the individual is everything. When a seeker has this knowledge, the perfect knowledge, "I am everything," arises automatically in him. He considers the entire world a playground where he can walk joyfully. Such a person, seeing equality, becomes liberated even while in the body. There is no doubt about this.

405.   *Anāhate pātrakarne'bhagnashabde sariddrute,*
         Shabdabrahmani nishnātah param brahmādhigacchati. [130]

---

129. Vasugupta, *Spanda Kārikā*, II-3.
130. *Vijñāna Bhairava*, 38.

> One who is steeped in *nāda* — which is the Absolute in the form of sound, which is the unstruck sound (*anāhata*) vibrating within, which can be heard only by the ear that becomes sensitive through yoga, which resounds uninterruptedly, and which rushes headlong like a river — attains the Absolute.

Just as the water of a stream flows continuously, in the same way, inside the body ten different kinds of subtle, unstruck sounds — great, mysterious, and unique music — go on spontaneously and unceasingly day in and day out. When this *nāda* ceases to vibrate in the body, one's last day has come; one's earthly passport expires, and one is taken to the cemetery. Throughout the universe, that divine sound has been vibrating from time immemorial. Even modern scientists believe that a mighty vibration is constantly reverberating. This is true. Once this vibration ceases, there will be a great deluge, and the world will become desolate. All men, women, mountains, and cities will merge into the void.

It is generally considered that sound cannot be created unless two objects are struck together. But the *nāda bhattāraka*, the Lord in the form of sound, is not produced in the body by the striking of one thing against another. Instead, it emanates spontaneously from the entire body. It constantly vibrates in every blood cell and in all of the seven elements. For this reason, it is called unstruck sound. Kabīr Sāhib wrote:

> *Gagan mandal me varshā hoyī*
> *ami ke kunda ulat gaye rī.*
> *Sataguru mile sāre dukha bisare,*
> *Antara ke pat khul gaye rī.*

In the inner space of the *sahasrāra*, the divine music is resounding. Because of that divine sound, nectar is released. I have become ecstatic from drinking it continuously. I have found the Sadguru. My inner divinity has been revealed to me, and all my pain has vanished.

To hear this sound, we have to make our ears sensitive. When two things are struck together on the outside, the ears perceive the sound, but the divine sound continually emanates within without anything being struck. Until the ears become sensitive through the practice of yoga, they cannot hear that divine sound. That sound is the Absolute in the form of sound.

When Kundalinī is awakened through the Guru's grace, she awards a prize to the yogi by ascending to the *sahasrāra* in the crown of the head and giving rise to ten different kinds of sounds. As a result of the Guru's gracious glance, the Goddess Kundalinī, the Divine Mother, manifests in the form of these sounds. The *mātrikā shakti*, which consists of all the letters of the alphabet, is said to be of the form of *nāda*. This is the divine sound, the music of the celestial beings. By releasing the nectar of inner love, it keeps a yogi in supreme bliss. This music is sublime. Compared to it, outer music is merely child's play.

As a Kundalinī yogi listens to the ten different sounds, he automatically recognizes the Absolute in the form of sound through the spontaneous practices of centering, meditation, and *samādhi*. A yogi who pursues the divine sound understands fully the nature of the Absolute in the form of sound and the place where the sound arises. He also understands the power of words and all the supernatural powers which arise from the groups of letters. *Nāda* issues from every pore of a yogi's body. If one wants to know why the great Siddhas chant, then one should understand these divine sounds through the practice of *nādānusandhāna*, the contemplation of the inner sound. Then one will know that *nāda* is God in manifest form. It is elixir. *Nāda* and chanting are nectarean.

A yogi also understands that from the Absolute in the form of sound, all four levels of speech — *parā, pashyantī, madhyamā,* and *vaikharī* — unfold. The principle of divine sounds unfolds from *parā* and *pashyantī* successively and proceeds to *madhyamā*. When the hearing turns inward through yoga and meditation, the divine sound is perceived. As a yogi turns within more and more, he hears the increasingly subtle levels of *nāda*. He fully understands the nature of the Absolute in the form of sound. When a seeker recognizes His nature, he effortlessly attains Parabrahman. When a yogi one-pointedly focuses his mind on the unstruck sound which resonates continuously, the true nature of the supreme space, which is Consciousness and luminosity, is revealed to him.

406.   *Yathā tathā yatra tatra*
         dvādashānte manaha kshipet,
         Prati kshanam kshīna vritter
         vailakshanyam dinair bhavet. [131]

> If a person fixes his mind on any one of the three *dvādashāntas* again and again, the fluctuation of his mind will diminish, and in a few days he will attain the state of Bhairava.

A yogi should take his consciousness, which arises spontaneously, through any one of the previously mentioned locations (the navel, the forehead, and so on) to the *dvādashānta* and try to focus his mind there. When he does this, the fluctuations of the mind diminish, its fickleness subsides, and at the right moment he experiences within himself the manifestation of the unique and extraordinary nature of Supreme Bhairava. Focusing the mind on the *dvādashānta* is a great and sublime practice, which I have explained in the

---

131. Ibid., 51.

book *I Am That.* It is often the case that when a person becomes upset, he lowers his head toward his heart and quietly breathes in and out. He finds a kind of stillness there. If he systematically practices focusing on the *dvādashānta,* then the attainment of supreme bliss is not far away. In fact, he will experience bliss immediately. This is one of the greatest and highest practices. It is the practice of the Siddhas.

God is *prakāsha* and *vimarsha.* Shaivism says that these are the form of Shiva. When a seeker meditates on this form of Shiva, he has the exalted experience of the Self. *Prakāsha,* illumination, arises in this experience.

407.   *Dhyātru dhyāne parityajya kramād dhyeyaika gocharam,*
       Nivāta dīpavacchittam samādhi rabhidhīyate. [132]

       When a person's practice becomes ripe, he gives up the idea of meditator as well as meditation. Then the mind makes the goal of meditation its subject and becomes still, like a flame where there is no wind.

This state of mind is called *samādhi.* The goal of meditation (*dhyeya*) is of the form of *prakāsha* and *vimarsha* and is the inner Witness. The thought-free state is called *samādhi.* The attainment of equality alone is the highest *samādhi.*

Lokānanda samādhi sukham[133] — "The delight that the yogi feels in abiding in his nature as the knower with respect to both the subject and the object in the world is his delight of *samādhi.*" The *Shiva Sūtras* say that if one has the awareness of the Self in all people, the idea of duality disappears and the state of unity which follows is the bliss of *samādhi.* Equanimity, stillness, one-pointedness, and the absence of thoughts and cares are all signs of the state of *samādhi.*

---

132. *Panchadashi,* I-55.
133. *Shiva Sūtras,* I-18.

From the standpoint of the Truth, the entire world is the embodiment of Shiva.

408.   *Sarvam deham chinmayam hi jagad vā pari bhāvayet,*
         Yugapan nirvikalpena manasa paramodayaha. [134]

         When, with a one-pointed and thought-free mind, a seeker contemplates his whole body or the entire universe all at once as being of the nature of Consciousness, he experiences the supreme awakening.

One should contemplate simultaneously every limb of the body from head to toe or the entire universe as the embodiment of Consciousness. In this kind of contemplation, when the mind becomes free of thoughts, the miracle of the mind's true nature is revealed within and without. Only light and nothing but light remains.

Saint Tukārām Mahārāj said that when the lotion of Consciousness was applied to his eyes, his vision became divine. He added that, in fact, the world has never existed as the world. Only Parabrahman exists. Tukārām realized Brahman in the form of *Om* or *So'ham.*

The illumined object, the body, and the world are not different from *prakāsha*, or light, which is the nature of the Supreme Principle. According to this theory, when the mind is free of thoughts and when all objects are transformed into light, the state of *paramodaya*, or supreme awakening, is revealed to a yogi.

Manasaha paramā gatihi — "The yogi's mind moves toward the Supreme." The *Shiva Sūtras* say, *Shuddha tattva sandhānād vā apashu shaktihi*[135] — "By constant awareness of the pure

---

134. *Vijñāna Bhairava*, 63.
135. *Shiva Sūtras*, I-16.

Principle, he becomes like one in whom the binding power which exists in the limited self is absent." The pure and perfect Principle is Paramashiva. He embodies the universe. By the practice of this awareness, the power of bondage is destroyed in a seeker. This is explained in the commentary on the *Spanda Kārikā* as follows:

> *Iti va yasya samvittihi krīdātvenākhilam jagat,*
> *Sa pashyan satatam yukto jīvanmukto na samshayaha.* [136]

The entire world is the play of the Universal Consciousness. One who sees it in this way becomes liberated while in the body.

He becomes Shiva. The world and human beings are composed of feeling. Through one's feeling, one can become anything.

409.   *Sarvam jagat svadeham vā svānanda bharitam smaret,*
         Yugapat svāmritenaiva parānanda mayo bhavet. [137]

The yogi should contemplate the entire universe or his own body all at once in its totality as being filled with his essential bliss. Then, through his own ambrosia-like bliss, he will become identified with the supreme bliss.

A person should feel himself to be full of the spontaneous inner bliss, which is different from the bliss experienced through objects outside the body in the world. This is a great centering technique; it is meditation as well as knowledge. One should never forget what Bahinabai said: "God and the world both exist according to one's feeling." The feeling of pure *vimarsha*, pure self-awareness, is the inner God. As a

---

136. Vasugupta, *Spanda Kārikā*, II-5.
137. *Vijñāna Bhairava*, 65.

yogi practices this awareness, he enters spontaneously into the natural state of bliss, which is like nectar and is described in the *Taittirīya Upanishad:*

> *Ānandādhyeva khalvimāni bhūtāni jāyante,*
> *Ānandena jātāni jīvanti.* [138]

> All individuals and beings, all things, whether sentient or insentient, matter or consciousness, arise from the blissful Supreme Principle.

Everything is born from the bliss of Consciousness, lives its life, and finally merges into the same Consciousness during the deluge. When a yogi attains the state of bliss, he becomes fulfilled and supremely blessed. Muktānanda says, "In reality, the entire world is the play of bliss. The appearance of the world depends on a person's vision. A person creates everything according to his feelings; he creates his own reality. What is day for a crow is night for an owl. What is day for an owl is night for a crow. Our own muddy vision creates our world. For God, only His world of bliss exists. If you practice God's viewpoint and attain your blissful inner sight, then no matter where you go there will be nothing but bliss and joy. The entire universe of men, women, creepers, trees, flowers, gardens, and the strumming of music surges with waves of bliss. Change your vision. You need do nothing else — the world of pain or pleasure is simply your own vision. Just turn within. Go deeper and deeper to where the state of perfect bliss and extraordinary ecstasy awaits you. When you reach that state, you will become it. You will know 'I am That.' "

410.   *Vāyudvayasya sanghattād antarvā bahir antataha,*
       Yogī samatva vijñāna samudgamana bhājanam. [139]

---

138. *Vijñāna Bhairava*, 64.
138. *Taittiriya Upanishad*, III-6-1.

By the fusion of the *prāna* and *apāna* [the *prāna* rising inwardly in the inner *dvādashānta*, or heart, the *apāna* rising externally in the outer *dvādashānta*], there finally arises a condition in which both *prāna* and *apāna* cease completely, whether in the inner or outer heart. By meditating on that condition of emptiness in which there is no awareness of either *prāna* or *apāna*, the yogi becomes so worthy that the intuitive experience of equality arises in him.

There is no *sādhanā* that can be compared to that of the *dvādashānta*. All Siddhas have attained God in the *dvādashānta* through So'ham. When a yogi has this equal vision, he understands the state of equality in which the dual state of *prāna* and *apāna* merges into the mysterious space, within or without. Along with that, in the same way, he dissolves all worldly objects into the mysterious Supreme Principle. Now he sees everything as inseparable from himself. By having this expanded vision of equality, he attains the supreme state.

411. *Samatā sarva devānām ovallī mantra varnayoho,*
      Āgamānām gatīnām cha sarvam shivamayam yataha. [140]

      The yogi who has attained the state of equality sees God alone in all deities, creepers, mantras, letters, revealed scriptural texts, actions, and phases.

      Samatā sarva bhāvānām vrittīnām chaiva sarvashaha,
      Samatā sarva drishtīnām dravyānām chaiva sarvashaha.
      Bhūmikānām cha sarvāsām ovallīnām tathaiva cha,
      Samatā sarva devānām varnānām chaiva sarvashaha.

      To see as equal all feelings, mental modifications, points of view, wealth, places, creepers, goddesses, and letters is called the vision of equality.

---

140. *Mahārtha Manjari.*

Abhinavagupta's *Tantrāloka* has made it clear that everything is Shiva. For this reason, it is very natural for the vision of equality to arise through the practice of this awareness. When everything is in fact Shiva, is it so difficult to see everything as Shiva? We should change our customary outlook. Then we will become happy.

412.   *Aham mamedam ityādi pratipatti prasangataha,*
         Nirādhare mano yāti tad dhyāna preranācchamī. [141]

Even when a person says, "I am," "This is mine," and so on, his thought goes to that absolute "I" which does not depend on any support. When he contemplates That, he attains lasting peace.

"This is me; this is mine" — the knowledge of this limited "I"-consciousness is actually not different from the knowledge of the perfect "I"-consciousness experienced by a wise person. Ultimately, the mind goes to that independent Principle because all knowledge of "I"-consciousness is woven together equally there. The essential nature of the Self is supreme bliss. It can never be divided. The knowledge of the perfect "I"-consciousness is this supreme bliss of God's essential nature. That perfect "I"-consciousness exists everywhere. Whether one is enlightened or ignorant, the Self of all is the same. Everyone loves his own Self. The love a person feels for his own Self can be considered to be worship of God.

Muktānanda says, "In the scriptures, love is considered to be God. Love is within all. Whoever loves himself loves God. That is worship, yoga and meditation. Moreover, love of the Self is also love of the world. It is the worship of the world as well as worship of all religions." Jagadguru Shankarāchārya said, *Ātmā tvam . . . pūjā te vishayopa bhoga rachanā –*

---

141. *Vijñāna Bhairava*, 131.

"O Lord, You are the Self of all. All the pleasures of my senses are objects for Your worship." What beautiful understanding! What a Shaivite teaching! Through knowledge, one can transform oneself. Becoming blissful, one can live on this earth in great ecstasy.

The knowledge of one's own Self cannot be considered to be either obscured or revealed since it does not depend on any concepts such as limitation or perfection. Whether a person is ignorant or enlightened, his true nature is bliss. The Self dwells as the embodiment of bliss and love in the hearts of both the ignorant and the enlightened. Therefore, Maheshwarānanda said that whether an individual has fallen into ignorance or is liberated, because of his essentially blissful nature he can never be separated from the supreme love of his own Self. As it is explained in a verse of the *Mahārtha Manjari*:

> *Nanvātmanaha priyārtham sarvasya*
> *priyatvam bhanati shrutihi,*
> *Tasmād ananda svabhāva*
> *ātmā muktop yamukto vā.*

Whether one is liberated or bound, one's essential nature, the Self, is always blissful.

Bliss exists in the form of the Self. The *shrutis* say, *Ātmanastu kāmāya sarvam priyam bhavati* — "Man loves all in order to fulfill his own desires." Everyone wants to remain in a state of happiness. Everyone wants to continue to exist. In this, a person's love for his own Self can be seen. There is no love greater than love for the Self. Because the nature of the Self is nothing but supreme bliss, one always thinks about bliss. Bhatta Utpaladeva says in the *Stotrāvali*:

> *Tvamevātmesha! Sarvasya sarvashchātmani rāgavān,*
> *Iti svabhāva siddham tvad baktim jānan jayej janaha.*

O independent Lord! You are the Self of all people.
Everyone loves his own Self. A devotee who has an
outlook of unity understands this devotion to You
which arises naturally, and he conquers the world.

All useful actions which are performed for the sake of the
Self are devotion to one's own Self. If one regards everything
from the right point of view, no one is ignorant, learned, or
enlightened. Only the independent God appears in all forms;
God alone exists in such concepts as ignorance, learning,
and enlightenment. One should become free of all thoughts
and serenely contemplate the essential nature of one's own
Self. There are not really different objects in this world. By
freeing the mind of thoughts, one should meditate on one's
own Self. In meditation, the mind becomes still. When this
happens, a seeker acquires a certain strength, and all his
conflicts vanish. He attains Shiva, the supreme *nirvāna*.
Shivatulyo jāyate — "He becomes like Shiva."

413. *Na me bandho na moksho me bhūtasyaitā vibhīshikāhā,*
Pratibimbam idam buddher jaleshviva vivasvataha. [142]

There is neither bondage nor liberation for me.
Bondage and liberation frighten only those who are
ignorant of their essential nature. The universe appears as a reflection in the intellect like the image of
the sun in water.

Such a yogi knows, "My nature is the embodiment of Consciousness. Since it is not divided by space, time, and so on, I
have not fallen into any bondage. I am the Self, which is
pure Consciousness. I do not have to free my Self from any
bondage." Bondage and liberation exist only when there is

---

142. Ibid., 135.

division. The ideas of bondage, liberation, and so on, apply only to a person who, because of *māyā*, does not understand his true nature and is afraid. He who wastes his life eating, drinking, playing, and watching movies and plays knows fear. He who is full of fear, misery, jealousy, enmity, and false pride experiences fear until death. He finds fearlessness and peace only when he is enclosed in a coffin and buried under cement and earth. The scriptures say, *Dvitīyādvai bhayam bhavati* — "When there is the notion of duality, there is fear." One who sees differences between the all-pervasive God, the world, and the Self spends his whole life in fear. A person who lacks knowledge eats fear throughout his life.

For a person who is terrified by duality, the ideas of bondage and liberation are like a scarecrow, a straw man which he takes to be real. For a yogi who understands that the totality of Consciousness and unity is the supreme goal, there is neither bondage nor liberation. He never thinks like this: "By perceiving people as other than himself, a person falls into bondage. He should avoid this and do what will liberate him instead. For this reason, he should certainly practice religious austerities." This type of discussion is mere imagination from the standpoint of the Truth. It is said, *Nistraigunye pathi vicharatām ko vidhihi ko nishedhaha* — "For a yogi who moves along the path which is beyond the three qualities, what dos and don'ts are necessary?" This means that such knowers of the Truth rise above precepts and prohibitions.

The fear of bondage and liberation cannot frighten an enlightened being. He realizes that just as the sun is seen reflected in water, the limited intellect is transformed into the notions "I am bound; I am liberated." From the intellect spring such notions as "What will happen to me? What will go wrong?" The conscious Self is beyond these. Therefore, a seeker should discard the limited intellect, which is full of such fearful ideas. Only then can he become established in his own natural state, the state of the Self. In reality, for an enlightened being, the seer, the seen, all activities, and all actions are knowledge. For him, there is neither virtue nor sin. A devotee says, "The One who pervades the universe makes me speak and act." The Lord says:

Prakāshamānam na prithak prakāshāt
sa cha prakāsho na prithag vimarshāt,
Nānyo vimarsho'hamiti svarūpād
ahamvimarsho'smi chidekarūpaha.

The illumined object is not different from *prakāsha*, illumination, and *prakāsha* is never different from *vimarsha*, the awareness of that which is illumined. This *vimarsha* is also not different from "I am," the essential nature of the Self. Therefore, I am that Principle, which is the conscious Self in the form of *vimarsha*.

This means that the knowledge of *prakāsha* is not different from the Self. That which is known is revealed through words and is not different from the means of knowing. Through the understanding of the oneness of that which is known and the means of knowing, a seeker becomes established in his own Self.

37

The Abode of the Self

414. In reality, out of its own happiness and out of love for its own blissful play, the one Truth has taken the form of the world. It creates the world, it is the world, yet it is different from the world. Even though it becomes everything and does everything, it still remains separate from everything. It embodies supreme wisdom. Why seek it? It is everything. Why look for it from house to house? It is everywhere. It flows as water. It sings as it blows in the wind. Becoming the earth, it supports everything. Becoming fire, it gives heat to everyone. It digests the food which we eat. It is the ether which fills the whole creation with space. Becoming the sun, it gives life to all plants. It is the stars. It is also men, women, boys, and girls, and it is Bhairava, Shrī Gurudev. By becoming all these things, it adorns the entire creation. At one place it takes birth, and at another place it dies.

Vijnāna Bodha Bhairava says, "I am everything. Whatever exists is Me. Whatever does not exist is also Me." If you want to understand this, learn it from these few words. There is no ignorance in you; there is no bondage, no sin, no anguish in you. Look within. There is Shiva, only Shiva. That alone is *vimarsha*, and That alone is *prakāsha*. O friends!

That is Rām, Rahīm, Shiva, God. There is nothing different from That.

The seer is reflected in the seen. Remember this. Experience within the wisdom of Bhairava, Shrī Gurudev. It is only *prakāsha*, the wisdom of Bhairava, which illumines everything from within, whether it is the mind, the intellect, the subconscious mind, or the ego. It is Shiva in the form of *vimarsha* who surveys from within everything which is illumined by *prakāsha* and knows all thoughts. Shiva is the entire cosmos in the form of *prakāsha* and *vimarsha*. Give up all involvements and entanglements. Stay where you are. All places belong to Shiva. In your own place, know your own Self as your Self. The independent "I" which exists within you is Shiva, the perfect "I." By strengthening this awareness, lose yourself in That. Lose yourself. To lose yourself is to find yourself. To seek yourself is to lose yourself. Understand this once and for all. There is no Shiva without you. Without Shiva, there is no you. This is the teaching of the experienced Siddhas. This is the abode of the Self. Here you can rest. This is where the saints dwell.

Īshwara Iyer was a great yogi who had practiced austerities. He was an enlightened Siddha Guru who had received the highest blessings through the compassion of the Sun God, the illuminer of all three worlds. The one who loved him above all was Nityānanda. Bhagawān Nityānanda was a born Siddha and a supreme *avadhūta*, perfect within himself. He was always engaged in his own duty of selfless service to humanity. Swami Muktānanda, who has received the gift of a small measure of his final grace, is the author of this work, which is Shaivism, the knowledge of the Self, and the essence of all scriptures. What is perfect now ends with perfection.

Swāmi Muktānanda Paramahamsa
Monday, July 7, 1980

GLOSSARY

Ābhāsa (*lit.* the shining forth): Appearance; emanation; manifestation; creation.

Ābhāsavāda: Theory of manifestation. The basic theory of Kashmir Shaivism. It explains the absolute freedom and autonomy of the Lord to manifest externally the world of names and forms, which always exists within Him. Accordingly, the world is the effect and Shiva is the cause. It is real, not an illusion as taught in Vedānta.

Abheda upāya: See *Shāmbhava upāya*.

Abhinavagupta (993-1015): Commentator and exponent of Kashmir Shaivism. Of the lineage of Vasugupta and Somananda, and author of *Tantrāloka* and *Ishwara Pratyabhijñā Vimarshini.*

Adhvā (*lit.* a course or path): According to Kashmir Shaivism, the whole universe in both its subjective and objective aspects is a proliferation of Shakti or *parāvāk* (subtle sound) in six forms known as the *shad adhvās*—the six routes or courses. They are, on the subjective side, *varna, mantra,* and *pada* and, on the objective side, *kalā, tattva,* and *bhuvana.* For more details, see Sir John Woodroffe, *The Garland of Letters* (Madras: Ganesh & Co., 1974).

Āgama Shastra: Divinely revealed scripture which has been handed down from teacher to pupil through the ages.

Aham (*lit.* "I"): "I"-Awareness; "I"-consciousness; the pure inner Self; the experiencing subject.

Aham vimarsha: Pure "I"-consciousness.

Anāhata nāda: The inner divine melody; the "unstruck" sound heard in meditation. See also *Nāda.*

Ānanda shakti: The power of absolute bliss.

Ānava mala: One of the impurities or limitations which brings about bondage of the universal Self and reduces it to a limited, individual being; the individual's innate ignorance of his true nature.

Ānava upāya: In Kashmir Shaivism, a means to Self-realization whereby the seeker uses his body, senses, *prāna* (breath), sound, etc.; also known as *bheda upāya* or *kriyā upāya*.

Anupāya: In Kashmir Shaivism, the path of "no means" to Self-realization; the subtlest means of Self-recognition, in which very little effort is made; also called *pratyabhijñā upāya*, since it consists of instant recognition of the true nature of the Self through Guru's grace.

Anusandhāna: Contemplation.

Āshram: A spiritual institution or community where spiritual discipline is practiced; the abode of a saint or holy man.

Asti (lit. exists): Existence; synonym for *sat*.

Ātmā-bala-sparsha: Inspiration coming from contact with the strength of the Self.

Avadhūta: A saint who lives in a state beyond body-consciousness and whose behavior is not bound by ordinary social conventions.

Bandha (lit. lock): Position practiced in Hatha Yoga. The three main locks are *jālandhara bandha*, in which the head is bent forward and the chin is pressed against the chest; *uddiyāna bandha*, in which the stomach muscles are pulled inward toward the spine; and *mūla bandha*, in which the anus is pulled inward.

Bhagawān: Lord; one who is glorious, illustrious, divine, venerable.

Bhairava: A name of Shiva meaning the Lord who is responsible for the creation, sustenance, and dissolution of the universe.

Bhairavi: The Shakti of Bhairava. See also Bhairava.

Bhāva: Feeling; attitude.

Bhedābheda: Unity in multiplicity.

Bhedābheda Advaitins: Followers of one of the subschools of Vedānta.

Bheda upāya: See *Ānava upāya*.

Bhogya or *bhojya*: The enjoyed object; object of experience.

Bhoktā: Enjoyer; subject; experiencer.

Bhūta-jaya: Control over the elements.

Bhūta-kaivalya: Withdrawal of the mind from the elements.

Bhūta-prithaktva: Separation from the elements.

Bhuvana adhvā: See *Adhvā*.

Bimba pratibimba: Original object and its reflection.

Bindu (*lit.* a dot, a point): The compact mass of Shakti gathered into an undifferentiated point, ready to manifest as the universe; a form made of light (Blue Pearl); the material cause and substance of creation.

Brahmā: The creator; one of the trinity of Brahmā, Vishnu, and Rudra.

Brahmādvaitins: Followers of the Vedas who consider nonbeing (*abhāva*) to be the fundamental principle. Their belief is based on the Upanishadic dictum that "all this was originally nonbeing." They accept the Void as the Ultimate Reality.

Brahman: Vedantic term for the Absolute Reality.

Brahmarandra: Subtle aperture in the crown of the head; the gateway of Brahman in the *sahasrāra*.

Buddhi: The ascertaining intelligence and the impersonal or superpersonal state of consciousness of a limited individual.

Chaitanya: The fundamental Consciousness which has absolute freedom of knowing (*jñāna shakti*) and doing (*kriyā shakti*).

Chakra (*lit.* wheel): In the human body, there are seven major energy centers or nerve plexes called *chakras*.

Chiti: See Chiti Shakti.

Chiti Shakti or Chitshakti: The dynamic power of the Absolute which manifests the world process.

Chit shakti: The power of self-revelation by which the Supreme shines by itself.

Chitta: In Kashmir Shaivism, the limitation of the Universal Consciousness manifested in the individual mind; the mind of the empirical individual. In Raja Yoga, *chitta* means mind, and in Vedānta, it refers to the subconscious.

Darshan: (1) Spiritual philosophy. (2) Seeing God, an image of God, or a holy being.

Dhyana: Meditation.

Dvādashānta: A point located at a distance of twelve fingers from various specific spots, such as the tip of the nose or the heart.

Eight supernatural powers (*siddhis*): Powers attained through mantra repetition, meditation, and other yogic practices. They are *anima*, the ability to reduce one's body to the size of an atom (used to travel in subtle realms); *mahimā*, the ability to expand the body to any size; *laghimā*, the ability to make the body light (levitation); *garimā*, the ability to make the body heavy; *prāpti*, the ability to attain everything; *prākāmya*, the ability to have one's wishes fulfilled; *īshatva*, the ability to gain lordship over everything; and *vashitva*, the power to attract and control all things.

Ekanāth Mahārāj (1528-1609): Householder poet-saint of Mahā- rāshtra. The illustrious disciple of Janārdan Swāmi, he was renowned in his later life for his scriptural commentaries and spiritual poetry.

Grāhaka: Perceiver; experiencer.

Grāhya: Objects of experience.

Guru: A spiritual master who has attained oneness with God and who initiates his disciples and devotees into the spiritual path and guides them to liberation.

Icchā shakti: The power of will of Paramashiva.

Icchā upāya: See *Shāmbhava upāya*.

Idam (*lit.* this): A technical word used in philosophy to denote the totality of the universe as well as any object of perception, gross or subtle.

Īshwara Pratyabhijnā Kārikā: One of the important works of Kash- mir Shaivism; written by Utpalāchārya, pupil of Somānanda, who combined the teachings of his master with philosophical reasoning.

Japa: Repetition of the mantra.

Jnāna shakti: The power of knowledge; the power of maintaining all objects in conscious relationship with oneself and with one another.

Jnāna upāya: See *Shākta upāya*.

Jnāneshwar Mahārāj (1275-1296): Foremost among the saints of Mahārāshtra and a child yogi of extraordinary powers. He was born in a family of saints, and his older brother Nivrittināth was his Guru. His verse commentary on the *Bhagavad Gītā*, the *Jnāneshwari*, written in the Marathi language, is acknowl- edged as one of the world's most important spiritual works. He took live *samādhi* at the age of 21 in Ālandi, where his *samādhi* shrine continues to attract thousands of seekers.

Kabīr (1440-1518): A great poet-saint who lived his life as a weaver in Benares. His followers were both Hindus and Mos- lems, and his influence was a strong force in overcoming religious factionalism.

Kala adhvā: See *Adhvā*.

Kanda: Egg-shaped, bulbous nerve plexus near the base of the spine.

Karana (*lit.* instrument): (1) The means of knowledge and action;

the inner and outer instruments (sense organs). (2) One of the practices in the *ānava upāya*, in which the aspirant contemplates the body and the nervous system as a replica of the cosmos.

Karma: Action; accumulation of past actions.

Kārma mala: One of the three impurities; limitation of the universal power of action to a finite power; impurity caused by the impressions left on the mind by one's *karma*, or motivated action.

Khecharī: Subspecies of *vāmeshvarī shakti*; one that moves in the *kha*, or space of Consciousness; also, the name of a Hatha Yoga technique.

Kriyā: Gross (physical) or subtle (mental, emotional) purificatory movement initiated by the awakened Kundalinī.

Kriyā shakti: The power of action; the power of Paramashiva to assume any and every form.

Kundalinī (*lit.* coiled one): The primordial Shakti, or cosmic energy, that lies coiled in the *mūlādhāra chakra* of every individual. When awakened, Kundalini begins to move upward within the *sushumnā*, the subtle central channel, piercing the *chakras* and initiating various yogic processes which bring about total purification and rejuvenation of the entire being. When Kundalinī enters the *sahasrāra*, the spiritual center in the crown of the head, the individual self merges in the universal Self and attains the state of Self-realization.

Levels of speech: See Speech, levels of.

Madhya (*lit.* central): The central, pure "I"-consciousness; the *sushumnā nādī*; also called *madhyadhāma*, the central abode.

Madhyamā: Sound in its subtle form as it exists in the mind/psyche before its gross manifestation.

Mādhyamikas: Followers of the Mādhyamaka school of Buddhism, which teaches that Reality lies in the middle (*madhyamā*) and not in any of the extremes. According to them, the world is unreal or void (*shūnya*), and all mental and nonmental phenomena are illusory. They are also called nihilists or Shūnyavādins.

Mahārāshtra: A state in western India.

Mala: Impurity; taint; limitation that hampers the freedom of Consciousness.

Mānasa Lake: A sacred lake on Mt. Kailāsa (Mt. Everest) where swans are said to migrate during the monsoon.

Mantra: Cosmic word or divine sound; a name of God.

Mantra adhvā: See *Adhvā*.

Mantra vīrya: The perfect "I"-consciousness, which is the fountainhead of all the powers or potencies behind the mantra; Shiva-consciousness; the experience of *pārāvak* (sound in its seed form).

Mātrikā: Letter or sound-syllable which is the basis of all words and hence of all knowledge; Shakti in sound form that manifests the universe. Because it is the source of words, *mātrikā* is said to be the source of ignorance (which comes about mainly through the ideas produced by words).

Mātrikā chakra: The Supreme Consciousness at the subtlest level of sound (*pārāvak*), consisting of the mantra of pure "I"-consciousness (*aham*). This mantra contains all the powers of sound (*mātrikās*) which bring into manifestation the world of diversity. See also *Mātrikā*.

Mātrikā shakti: The power of sound; a form of the Universal Consciousness.

Māyā: The force which shows the unreal as real and presents that which is temporary and short-lived as eternal and everlasting. In the Advaita Vedānta of Shankarāchārya, it is described as the beginningless cause which brings about the illusion of the world; an indescribable power of Brahman, which is neither real nor totally unreal. See also *Māyā shakti* and *Māyā tattva*.

Māyā pramātā: The individual bound soul governed by *māyā*.

Māyā shakti: The Shakti of Shiva who creates differentiation in the mind of the bound soul and gives rise to *māyā tattva*; the limiting power of the Infinite; also called *mahā māyā*. See also *Māyā tattva*.

Māyā tattva: The principle that throws a veil over pure Consciousness; material cause of physical manifestation; source of the five *kanchukas*, or limitations. See also *Māyā shakti*.

Māyīya mala: The limitation caused by *māyā* which gives rise to the individual soul, its gross and subtle bodies, and brings about a sense of differentiation.

Mudrā: (1) Mud (joy), *ra* (to give); called *mudrā* because it gives the bliss of the Self. (2) Seal, because it seals up (*mudranāt*) the universe into the being of transcendental Consciousness. (3) Hatha Yoga posture and manipulation of different organs of the body as an aid in concentration. (4) Symbolic signs made with the fingers in ritualistic worship and classical dance.

Mudrā vīrya: The power by which one experiences the emergence of the supreme "I"-consciousness; also called *mantra vīrya* or *khecharī* state.

Mūlādhāra: Spiritual center at the base of the spine where the Kundalinī lies dormant.

Nāda: (1) Metaphysically, the first movement of Shiva-Shakti toward manifestation. (2) In yoga, the unstruck sound experienced in meditation.

Nādānusandhāna: A practice in which one listens to the inner divine melodies.

Nādī: Channel in the subtle body through which the vital force flows.

Nādī samhāra: Dissolution of *prāna* and *apāna* into the *sushumnā*.

Nāmadev (1270-1350): A poet-saint of Pandharpur in Mahārāshtra who composed thousands of devotional songs, many of which glorify the repetition of the divine name.

Nārada: A divine *rishi*, or seer; a great devotee and servant of Vishnu. He appears in many of the Purānas and is the author of the *Nārada Bhakti Sūtras*, the authoritative text on Bhakti Yoga.

Nirnaya (*lit.* establishing): Confirmation.

Nirvikalpa samādhi: Superconscious thought-free state.

Nirvisheshadvaitins: Followers of one of the subschools of nondualism.

Nishkala: The transcendental Principle which is beyond all manifestation and limitation.

Nishyanda: Vibration; throb.

Niyamana (*lit.* checking): Punishing; restraining; subduing; binding.

Nyāya: One of the six main philosophies of Hinduism; based on logic.

Om Namah Shivāya: A mantra meaning "Salutations to Shiva." Shiva denotes the inner Self. It is known as the great redeeming mantra because it has the power to grant worldly fulfillment as well as spiritual realization.

Pancha kanchukas (*lit.* five cloaks): The limitations or coverings of the individual soul; by-products of *māyā*. They are *kalā*, which brings about limitation of the power to do; *vidyā*, which brings about limitation of the power of knowledge; *rāga*, which reduces the completeness of the Universal Consciousness and brings about the desire for particular things; *kala*, which reduces the eternality of Universal Consciousness and brings about limitation of time; *niyati*, which brings about limitation of cause, space, and form.

Pāramārthika: The Ultimate; the Supreme; spiritual.

Paramashiva: The Ultimate Reality; the core of all.

Parasāmvit: Supreme Consciousness, in which there is complete fusion of *prakāsha* and *vimarsha*; the supreme "I"-consciousness. See also *Prakāsha* and *Vimarsha*.

Prakāsha (*lit.* light): The principle of Self-revelation; the principle by which everything is known.

Prakriti: Primordial nature; the basic stuff of the material world. In Kashmir Shaivism, *prakriti* is identified with Shakti.

Pramāna: Knowledge; means of knowledge; proof.

Pramātri or *pramātā*: Knower; subject; experiencer.

Prameya: Known; object of knowledge; object.

Pramiti or *miti*: Right cognition (free of error).

Prāna: Vital force; specifically, the vital air in the breathing process.

Prāna shakti: Life force; the supreme energy in the form of *prāna*.

Pratibhā: (1) Ever-creative activity of Consciousness. (2) The spontaneous supreme "I"-consciousness. (3) Parashaktī.

Prātibhāsika: Apparent; illusory.

Pravrittivāda: Theory of extroverted life; seeing God while living in the world.

Pūrnāhantā: The supreme "I"-consciousness; the nonrelational perfect "I"-consciousness.

Puryashtaka (*lit.* the city of the group of eight): The five *tanmatras* (sound, touch, color, taste, and smell), *buddhi* (intellect), *ahamkāra* (ego), and *manas* (mind); another name for the subtle body.

Rasa: Taste; juice; elixir.

Sādhu: Holy being.

Sahaja: Innate essential nature; natural.

Sahajavidyā: Knowledge of the innate essential nature; state of pure, divine Consciousness in which mental awareness ceases; pervasion into Shiva-consciousness (*Shiva-vyāpti*).

Sahasrāra: Thousand-petaled spiritual center at the crown of the head where one experiences the highest states of consciousness.

Sakala: All limited individual souls or experiencing subjects.

Sāmānya (*lit.* ordinary): General; common.

Samavesha: Absorption or merging of the individual consciousness into the Universal Consciousness.

Samvit: Universal Consciousness.

Sānkarya: Mixture.

Savisheshādvaitins: Followers of one of the subschools of Vedānta.

Senses of perception: The five senses of perception, or *jnānendriyas*, are the power of hearing (*shrotra*), the power of feeling by touch (*tvak*), the power of seeing (*chakshu*), the power of tasting (*jihvā*), and the power of smelling (*ghrāna*).

Seven experiencers: Due to the different positions occupied by Consciousness in the process of its manifestation of the universe, its outlook changes at seven different levels. Its technical names at these seven stages are *Shiva pramatā, mantra maheshwara, manteshwara, mantra, vijñānākala, pralāyākala,* and *sakala.* The universe can be experienced at any of these seven levels.

Seven pentads: This can be interpreted as $7 \times 5 = 35$ or as $7 + 5$. If seven pentads are taken to be thirty-five, they represent the thirty-five *tattvas* from Shiva to the earth. If taken to be $7 + 5$, seven represents the seven experiencers and five represents the five *shaktis: chit, ānanda, icchā, jnanā,* and *kriyā.* Five also refers to the five *kanchukas.* See also Seven experiencers and *Pancha kanchukas.*

Shākta upāya: In Kashmir Shaivism, a means to Self-realization, primarily through the use of the mind. Since mental activity plays a vital role in it, it is also called *jnāna upāya,* or the path of knowledge; also called *bhedābheda* (unity in multiplicity) *upāya.*

Shakti (Chiti, Kundalinī, Kundalinī Shakti): The divine cosmic power which projects, maintains, and dissolves the universe.

Shakti: Power; force; energy.

Shakti chakra: The group of powers which control the inner and outer worlds.

Shaktipāt: Transmission of spiritual power (Shakti) from the Guru to the disciple; spiritual awakening by grace.

Shāmbhava upāya: In Kashmir Shaivism, a means to Self-realization meant for advanced aspirants; sudden emergence of Shiva-consciousness by a mere hint from the Guru. Since in this *upāya* the Self is realized through the will, it is also called *icchā upāya.*

Shiva: (1) A name for the all-pervasive Supreme Reality. (2) One of the Hindu trinity; represents God as the destroyer; the personal God of the Shaivites. In his personal form, he is portrayed as a yogi wearing a tiger skin and holding a trident, with snakes coiled around his neck and arms.

Shiva drishti (*lit.* vision or outlook of Shiva): (1) A name for the Shaivite philosophy. (2) Name of the treatise on Kashmir Shaivism by Somānanda, the first exponent after Vasugupta.

Shrīmad Bhāgavatam: The most popular devotional scripture in India, containing many legends, stories, and the life and teachings of Krishna; composed by Vyāsa.

Shrutis: Sacred works.

Shuddha adhvā: See *Adhvā*.

Shuddhavidyā: (1) Pure knowledge. (2) The *tattva* immediately above the level of material manifestation.

Shūnyāvādins: Followers of one of the subschools of Vedānta.

Siddha: A perfected yogi; one who has attained the highest state and become one with God.

Siddha Yoga: The yoga which takes place spontaneously within a seeker whose Kundalinī has been awakened by a Siddha Guru and which leads to the state of spiritual perfection.

Spanda: Creative pulsation; apparent motion in the motionless Shiva which brings about the manifestation, maintenance, and withdrawal of the universe; the independent (*svātantrya*) Shakti.

Speech, levels of: Sound originates in the deepest level of unmanifest Consciousness, the *parā* level. From here, it arises successively through the *pashyantī* level to the *madhyamā* (subtle) level of speech until it manifests on the gross level as *vaikharī*, or articulated speech. The four levels of speech correspond to the four bodies—the *vaikharī* to the gross body, *madhyamā* to the subtle body, *pashyantī* to the causal body, and *parā* to the supracausal body.

Sthānakalpanā: One of the practices in the *anava upaya*, whereby one concentrates on external objects.

Svarūpa: One's own or essential nature.

Swāmi: Title of a *sannyāsin*.

Tanmatras: The subtle essences of sound, touch, sight, taste, and smell from which the five gross elements are formed.

Tattva (*lit.* that-ness): That which is the essence of each stage of manifestation (see footnote 47). The process of creation, according to Kashmir Shaivism, contains thirty-six *tattvas*: Shiva, Shakti, Sadāshiva, Īshwara, *shuddhavidyā, māyā tattva*, the five cloaks (*pancha kanchukas*), *purusha* (individual soul), *prakriti* (primordial nature, the basic stuff of the material universe), *buddhi* (intellect), *ahamkāra* (ego), *manas* (mind), the five powers of sense perception, the five powers of action, the five *tanmatras*, or rudimentary elements, and the five gross elements. These comprise creation from Shiva to the earth. For more information, see *Introduction to Kashmir Shaivism* (Oakland, California: SYDA Foundation, 1978).

Three worlds: Heaven, hell, and the world of mortals; the states of waking, dream, and deep sleep.

Tukārām Mahārāj (1608-1650): Great poet-saint of Mahārāshtra; author of thousands of *abhangas* (devotional songs).

Tulasidās (1532-1623): North Indian poet-saint and author of *Rāmacharitamānas*, the life story of Lord Rāma written in Hindi, which is still one of the most popular scriptures in India.

Turīya or *turya* (*lit.* fourth): The fourth state of consciousness beyond the states of waking, dreaming, and deep sleep and pervading all the states; identified with the Self.

Ucchāra: In the *āṇava upāya*, a technique of concentration on the *prāna shakti*, or vital force. Various aspects of *ānanda* (bliss) are experienced during this concentration.

Unmanā or *unmanī* (*lit.* that which transcends *manas*, or mind): The transcendental Shakti of Paramashiva in its primal movement toward manaifestation. This Shakti is *amātra*, or measureless and beyond time.

Unmesha (*lit.* opening of the eye): (1) The externalizing of the *icchā shakti*; the beginnning of the world process. (2) Unfolding of the spiritual awareness.

Upāya: Means; technique.

Vaisheshika: One of the six major philosophies of Hinduism, which expounds the theory that everything is made of atoms.

Varna: Letter of the alphabet; in the *āṇava upāya*, an object of concentration known as *nāda*.

Vedas: The highest authoritative scriptures of India; very ancient revealed scriptures.

Vibhūti: Splendor; power; greatness.

Vijnānavādins: Followers of one of the schools of Buddhism, which holds that external objects are unreal. That which appears to be external is actually an idea in the mind. However, the mind is real. This view is called subjective idealism (*vijnānavāda*). Vijnānavādins are also called Yogāchāras.

Vimarsha: The Self-consciousness or Self-awareness of Paramashiva, full of *jnāna* and *kriyā*, which brings about the world process. On an individual level, the aspect of consciousness through which one understands the specific characteristics of that which is known.

Vīresha: The lord of the senses, who has experienced the delight of the transcendental state of consciousness.

Vishishtādvaitins: Followers of Rāmānuja's "qualified monism," the main theory of which is that God is the only reality.

Within Him there exist as parts the different unconscious (*achit*) material objects as well as the many conscious (*chit*) souls.

Vivartavādins: Followers of the Vedānta of Shankarāchārya. This school holds that because of *māyā*, the Ultimate Reality appears as something other than itself, like a rope appearing as a snake.

Void: (1) The state of nothingness experienced in deep sleep. (2) The state of the formless Absolute. According to the Buddhists, this is a state of nonexistence. In Kashmir Shaivism, however, Void is emptiness in the sense that it is without manifest creation. It is not a state of nonexistence, because it has the nature of being, consciousness, and bliss.

Vyāvahārika sattā: Empirical reality, which is limited in space and time.

Yoga (*lit.* union): The state of oneness with the Self, God; the practices leading to that state.

Yogāchāras: See Vijnānavādins.

Yogi: One who practices yoga; one who has attained the goal of yoga.

Yoginī: A female practitioner of yoga.

INDEX

Ābhāsas, 105–107, 146, 148, 151. *See also* Manifestation
Ābhāsavāda, 105–107
Abheda upāya. See Shāmbhava upāya
Abhinavagupta, 107, 124, 202. *See also Ishwara Pratyabhijñā Vimarshinī; Tantrāloka; Tantrasāra*
Absolute: bliss of, 27, 68; and the experience of a Siddha, 27, 51, 54, 61; in the form of sound, 194-196; "I am the Absolute," 54, 127; as individual soul, 3, 56, 58; in Kashmir Shaivism and the world, 121; and Kundalinī Shakti, 10; in Vedantic teachings, 127, 170. *See also* Supreme Reality
Actions, 172; fivefold, 18 n. 10, 19, 84, 100–101, 118, 154, 177; and four bodies, 77; fruits of, 6, 15, 55, 57, 75, 123, 132–133, 135; and limited knowledge, 75, 123, 133; right understanding of, 122–123, 132, 139-140, 204; and the Self, 3–4, 75, 123, 206; toward Self-realization, 60, 190, 192, 196-201, 205; and Shakti Kundalinī, 10; and *shaktipāt*, 15; as Shiva, 129, 166; of Siddhas, 24–25, 36–37, 50; and *spanda*, 156, 159, 160, 166. *See also Gunas; Karma; Kriyā shakti*
Addictions, 62–63; of Baba, 65–67

Adhvā, 90. *See also Shuddha adhvā*
Adoni Lakshmībāi, 43–44
Adornment, 63
Advaita, 120–121
Advaita philosophy, 119–125
Advaitavādins, 121
Āgama Shastras, 152, 181. *See also* Scriptures
Agitation, 15, 84, 117, 128
Aham, 4, 91, 139, 188; *Aham brahmāsmi*, 127; *Aham vimarsha*, 164, 206; and the *spanda* principle, 160, 162. *See also* "I"-consciousness
Ahamtā, 162
Akkamahādevi, 47
Ālandi, 44
Allāh, 119
Anāhata. See Nāda
Ānanda, 11, 77, 100. *See also* Bliss
Ānanda shakti, 11, 100
Ānava (bheda/kriyā) upāya, 72, 73, 88–95, 96. *See also Upāyas*
Ānava mala, 75, 122, 123, 134
Anupāya (Guru kripā upāya), 96-97
Aparokshānubhūti, 167, 168–169. *See also* Shankarāchārya; *Vedānta*
Arjuna, 55, 174
Asānkarya, 148
Āshram, 32, 33, 85
Ātma. See Self

221

232

OTHER PUBLICATIONS

By Swami Muktānanda

Play of Consciousness Muktānanda's spiritual autobiography
Satsang With Baba (Five Volumes) Questions and answers
Getting Rid of What you Haven't Got Informal interviews and talks
Muktānanda-Selected Essays Edited by Paul Zweig
Meditate Muktānanda's basic teaching on meditation
In the Company of a Siddha Muktānanda talks with pioneers in science,
consciousness and spirituality
Reflections of the Self Poems of spiritual life
Light on the Path Essential aspects of the Siddha Path
Siddha Meditation Commentaries on the Shiva Sūtras and other ancient texts
Mukteshwari I & II Poetic aphorisms
I Am That The science of Hamsa mantra
Kundalinī The Secret of Life Muktānanda's teachings on our innate sprirtual energy
I Welcome You All With Love "Little book" of aphorisms
God Is With You "Little book" of aphorisms
A Book for the Mind Aphorisms on the mind
I love You Aphorisms on love
To Know The Knower Aphorisms on the highest knowledge
Sadgurunath Mahariaj Ki Jaya Photos and essays from Muktānanda's 1974
Australian tour
What is an Intensive? Muktānanda's 2-day program for spiritual awakening
Bhagawan Nityānanda Portrait of Muktānanda's Guru, Bhagawan Nityānanda

Other Books
Introduction to Kashmir Shaivism The philosophy most closely reflecting
Muktānanda's teaching
Understanding Siddha Yoga, Volumes I & II Textbooks on Siddha Yoga

About Swami Muktānanda
A Search for the Self by Swami Prajnananda. Swami Muktānanda's biography

If you want more information about these books, write to
SYDA Bookstore, P.O. Box 605, South Fallsburg, N.Y. 12779

DIRECTORY OF MAJOR CENTERS AND ASHRAMS

There are over 250 Siddha Yoga Meditation Centers and residential Ashrams around the world. They all hold regular programs which are free and open to the public. Many of them also conduct Siddha Yoga Meditation Intensives and Introductory Programs. Contact any of the following major centers for the location of the center nearest you.

Gurudev Siddha Peeth
P.O. Ganeshpuri (Pin 401 206)
Dist. Thana, Maharashtra, India

Shree Gurudev Ashram
Village Bhatti
Mehrauli Block, New Delhi South
India 110 030

**Siddha Yoga Dham
Oakland**
P.O. Box 11071
Oakland, California 94611
1107 Stanford Avenue
Oakland, California 94608
Phone: (415) 655-8677

**Siddha Yoga Dham
Ann Arbor**
1520 Hill
Ann Arbor, Michigan 48104
Phone: (313) 994-5625

**Siddha Yoga Dham
Manhattan**
324 West 86th Street
New York, New York 10024
Phone: (212) 873-8030

**Siddha Yoga Dham
Los Angeles**
605 S. Mariposa
Los Angeles, California 90005
Phone: (213) 386-2328

Siddha Yoga Dham Boston
Fernwood Road, Manor House
Chestnut Hill, Mass. 02167
Phone: (617) 734-0137

Siddha Yoga Gainesville
1004 SW First Avenue
Gainesville, Florida 32601
Phone: (904) 375-7629

**Siddha Yoga Dham
Philadelphia**
6429 Wayne Avenue
Philadelphia, Pennsylvania 19119
Phone: (215) 849-0888

**Siddha Yoga Dham
Houston**
3815 Garott
Houston, Texas 77006
Phone: (713) 529-0006

Siddha Yoga Dham Miami
P.O. Box 52-3464
Miami, Florida 33152
256 S.W. 12th Street
Miami, Florida 33130
Phone: (305) 261-8924

Siddha Yoga Dham Seattle
1409 N.E. 66th
Seattle, Washington 98115
Phone: (206) 523-2853

**Siddha Yoga Meditation
Ashram Chicago**
2100 W. Bradley Place
Chicago, Illinois 60618
Phone: (312) 327-0536

**Siddha Yoga Dham
Washington, D.C.**
1834 Swann Street N.W.
Washington, D.C. 20009
Phone: (202) 667-0842,
(202) 483-4849

Siddha Yoga Dham Hawaii
P.O. Box 10191
Honolulu, Hawaii 96816
3807 Diamond Head Circle
Honolulu, Hawaii 96815
Phone: (808) 732-1558

**Muktananda Meditation
  Center Vancouver**
P.O. Box 2990, Vancouver, B.C.
V6B 3X4 Canada
Phone: (604) 734-7181

**Siddha Yoga Dham
  Melbourne**
202 Gore Street, Fitzroy
Melbourne VIC 3065 Australia
Phone: (03) 419-6950

Siddha Yoga Dham London
1 Bonneville Gardens
London SW 4 England
Phone: (01) 675-4105

**Siddha Yoga Dham
  München**
Fasangartenstr. 125, D-8000
München 90, Federal Republic
  Germany
Phone: (089) 683-414

Siddha Yoga Dham France
153 Rue du Faubourg Saint Denis
Paris 75010 France
Phone: (3) 952-7004

**Muktananda Siddha
  Meditation Center Bern**
Brunngasse 54, 3011
Bern, Switzerland
Phone: (031) 22. 59. 63

I dedicate this book to the lotus feet of my supreme father, Sadguru Bhagawan Nityananda, to whom I owe my existence.